UNQUOTE

UNQUOTE

Derek Lambert

Arlington Books
Clifford Street Mayfair
London

UNQUOTE
first published 1981 by
Arlington Books (Publishers) Ltd
3 Clifford Street Mayfair
London W.1.

© *Derek Lambert 1981*

Set in England by
Inforum Ltd, Portsmouth
Printed and bound in England by
Billing & Sons Ltd
Guildford, Worcester and London

British Library Cataloguing in Publication Data
Lambert Derek
Unquote.
1. Authors, English — 20th century — Biography
2. Journalists — Great Britain — Biography
I. Title
070'.92'4   PR6062.A47Z/

ISBN 0 85140 543 6

For Guy and Marjorie

AUTHOR'S NOTE

The danger of writing a light-hearted account of life in Russia is that the author may be accused of concocting a defence of Soviet repression; employing a diversionary tactic, that is. Let it be firmly stated here that, during my one-year sojourn in Moscow, I became fully aware of all the reprehensible aspects of the Kremlin regime.

Nevertheless, beneath this umbrella of despotic rule, humour and zest still abound among the Russian people, a phenomenon rarely recorded by the chroniclers of Soviet affairs whose pens seem to be guided by the dark spectres of the Russian Legend. In this book I have attempted both to put that particular record straight and to provide a carefree account of life behind the Iron Curtain, unencumbered by analysis or doom-laden prognostications.

UNQUOTE

I

Within one hour of my arrival in Moscow I saw a car burst into flames; within two a KGB agent had collapsed unconscious at my feet; within four I was gazing nervously at a set of pornographic photographs featuring a bored-looking girl and a man wearing only his socks.

So it was all true what they had told me about Life Behind the Iron Curtain. Instant violence and Machiavellian intrigue rounded off with an attempt to compromise me! And only a couple of months earlier — in July, 1966 — I had been quartered at the Norfolk Hotel in Nairobi, sipping whisky sours with white hunters and admiring the golden-limbed air stewardesses cushioning the swimming pool.

Admittedly I was restless after two years in Africa as the *Daily Express* staff reporter there. The initial impact of my big story, Rhodesia's Unilateral Declaration of Independence, was beginning to wane, and in Kenya I had been covering an indifferent story about elephants. Where next? I wondered, watching a bevy of gorgeous East African Airlines hostesses replace a quartet of Amazonian El Al girls. New York? Paris? A more turbulent corner of Africa, perhaps . . .

The telephone at the bar rang and I was summoned to the telex in the centre of the city where, it was euphemistically stated, an important message awaited me. The message was from David English, the dashing foreign editor of the *Express*, subsequently editor of the *Daily Mail*, and it bruised my senses as surely as a declaration of war.

I was ordered to return to my base in Salisbury, clear up my affairs and fly back to London *to await a posting to Moscow*.

In Rhodesia, a country still definitely optimistic about its white-orientated future, I paid my bar bills, sold my rusty little Morris 1000 for twenty pounds, and bade farewell to my friend and mentor, Mike Keats of UPI, and his wife, Sybil, who both envisaged Moscow as a mere stepping-stone to Siberia.

Back in London the long wait for the necessary documents to work in the Soviet Union began. But, paradoxically, the tedium while the Russians checked out my life back to the womb, sharpened my appetite for whatever lay ahead. The posting was, after all, something of an accolade in an accident-prone career that had begun on the *Dartmouth Chronicle* and survived thirteen years on the *Daily Mirror* and the *Express*. And a challenge — because the occupational disease of reporters based in Moscow seemed to be nervous breakdowns.

To prepare myself I took a crash course on vodka consumption in the Fleet Street pubs, tossing back the fire-water with wild-eyed abandon and hurling the occasional glass against the wall.

Finally, I was fully accredited; the fact that I didn't speak a word of Russian had apparently favourably impressed the Soviet authorities. And one blue and gold autumn day I took off from Heathrow on a Ilyushin-104 bound for Moscow.

At Sheremetyevo airport I was met by Robin Stafford, a very large, very smooth and very professional correspondent who had been posted to Rome. He was exceedingly kind to me, his successor, but his imperious air of authority was daunting: I couldn't see myself emulating it. We navigated customs and immigration without trouble. One official asked

10

me if I possessed any gold; I pointed at one of my back teeth and grimaced to indicate that I was making a joke. No-one laughed.

By now it was dusk with an edge of cold in the air. Robin led me to the *Express'* grey Cortina parked outside. I was struck first by the scarcity of cars on the road, then by the scarcity of windscreen-wipers on the cars. "All been nicked," Robin explained. "We'll have to take ours off tonight if we want to keep them."

We drove past dead-eyed apartment blocks and copses of silver birch. Cyclists and pedestrians, already wearing spaniel-eared fur hats although the snow hadn't yet arrived, stared curiously at our bourgeois car. Apprehension, nourished by a diet of espionage fiction, stirred inside me. Were our movements, even now, being charted by potato-faced men with binoculars and pistols in their holsters?

At that moment the car in front of us, a maroon Moskvich, burst into flames. A missile intended for our Cortina? "What do you think happened?" I asked tentatively.

"God knows," said Robin, as if it happened all the time — we learned later that leaking petrol had ignited — and steered the car into a driveway leading to a magnificent dacha.

The walls inside were covered with split pine imported from Canada and hung with icons. Russian music as sad as autumn issued from stereo loudspeakers. A party was in progress and champagne, vodka and caviar awaited us on the sideboard. Hardly the Russia I had been led to expect by authors fulminating about the poverty of Soviet life, the wretched food in the restaurants and the lack of bath-plugs in the hotels.

All Robin had told me was that the owner of the dacha was a useful contact. His name was Vitali Yevgennevich Lui, better known as Victor Louis, but what Robin had omitted to tell me was that he was a KGB contact. He was a slender, dreamy sort

11

of man in his late thirties who spoke English with a slight American drawl. He was the Kremlin's chief agent of disinformation, a profession that didn't preclude him from pulling off genuine scoops such as Khrushchev's plunge from favour.

In Europe it was the London *Evening News*, the newspaper he represented in Moscow, which benefited most from his knowledge of Kremlin intrigue; but from time to time most of the correspondents were given a Louis exclusive. Most of them, that is, except the correspondents of such Communist newspapers as the *Morning Star*.

All such journalists received niggardly assistance from the fount of their ideology. I can think of only two reasons to account for this churlish behaviour on the part of the Russians. Firstly, they saw no point in preaching to the converted; and secondly, they had little respect for newspapers whose content was as abysmal as their own.

But I had formed no such theories as I chatted warily to my soft-voiced, soft-haired host who had, it seemed, travelled the world as freely as a Queen's Messenger. Surely Soviet citizens had to possess a sheaf of documents to cross the road?

Louis offered me champagne, vodka or even Johnnie Walker Black Label whisky if I preferred it. Remembering the horrendous effect vodka had wrought on me in Fleet Street when I had been led howling into the night, I asked him if he had any beer. Robin moaned gently to himself but Louis took it like a man.

After a few conversational niceties Louis introduced me to a journalist from the Novosti Press Agency which I knew to be affiliated to the KGB. He was a bulky fellow with a frown stitched into his forehead and I greeted him civilly: "Good evening, how are you?"

His response was alarming. He grabbed a glass of vodka, shouted "*Nasdarovya,*" downed the drink and collapsed in an

12

untidy heap at my feet.

Louis apologised. It was not, apparently, the Novosti representative's first drink. Louis was visibly concerned because newly-accredited correspondents often reported to their newspapers their first impressions of Moscow. Although these stories were carried only in early editions to indulge the reporter in his claustrophobic outpost, it was not an auspicious start to the Soviet PR operation.

The journalist, Louis told me, had suffered a bereavement. Why that should make him attend a party and down the best part of a bottle of vodka wasn't explained; nevertheless, I tacitly agreed not to mention the incident.

Stepping over the unconscious mourner, Robin and I left to continue our journey towards the unknown. This proved to be a complex of apartment blocks looming against the night sky, surrounded by a penitentiary-style wall and guarded by militia wearing blue uniforms and grey coats. My home!

It was, in fact, one of several such complexes built exclusively for foreign journalists and diplomats, each a multi-lingual ghetto, which only privileged Russians were allowed to enter. Ours stood on Kutuzovsky Prospect, named after the marshal who routed Napoleon. Our address was no. 15; Brezhnev lived at no. 28.

Robin parked the Cortina in a brightly-lit courtyard, like a set from a POW escape film and, sharing the lift with a Cuban — "Those poor buggers get all the stick from the Russians," remarked Robin as though the morose-looking Man from Havana was stone deaf — we made a shuddering ascent to the *Express* apartment.

This was an enormous place. Stark, yet lived-in. It seemed to have two of most things and Robin explained that this was because it was two flats knocked into one. I inspected a long corridor, an office stacked with obscure reference books, two antiquated bathrooms inhabited by cockroaches as quick and

13

stealthy as lizards, a cubicle where a Tass machine chattered agitatedly away, a kitchen with a saucepan of borsch bubbling on the stove, a couple of bedrooms with disrobing wall-paper . . .

From the lounge I heard Robin's voice. No-one had entered the flat since our arrival. Had he carefully saved his breakdown for my opening night? Distinctly I heard the memorable words: "Good evening, Fred. All right tonight, my old tulip?"

When I went into the lounge I found him addressing the main light-fitting. I was about to withdraw discreetly when he noticed me and said, "That's the only way to treat them."

"Them?"

"Our friends."

"You mean the bugs?"

He shrugged. "Call 'em what you like. But I like to keep up a healthy relationship with them. Sometimes I tell them to get stuffed. Don't I, Fred?" he said to the light-fitting.

Somewhere, I supposed, a sinister figure wearing ear-phones was nodding forlornly.

All the correspondents, Robin told me, had their own ways of combatting the KGB eavesdroppers. Some turned up the radio and whispered furtively to each other to the accompaniment of the Red Army Band; others waited until they were out-of-doors to impart gems of clandestine infor-mation; a few swopped secrets in their cars, failing to appreci-ate that their cars were probably as thoroughly bugged as their apartments.

After I had absorbed all this sinister information, Robin showed me a sugared red-currant lying under the television set. "It's been there for eight months," he said. "We want to see when the maid finally gets round to sweeping under the telly."

Then he departed to keep an appointment, and I was left nervously patrolling my new domain — which was when I

14

found the pornographic pictures in the drawer of a table in the spare bedroom where I was to sleep until Robin left.

For a moment I stared numbed at the young man wearing nothing but his socks — odd ones — about to impale a blonde who looked as though she would rather be playing Bingo. Obviously the photographs had been planted. The front door would be kicked down and I would be accused of trying to import filthy pictures into the Soviet Union. I returned the photographs to their envelope, slipped this inside my jacket and slunk down to one of the ancient bathrooms. As I switched on the light the cockroaches made a run for it.

First, I tried to burn a picture of the girl holding the man's member as though it were a stale bread-roll. I struck a match and applied it to one corner, assuming naively that the photograph would vanish in a sheet of flame. It did no such thing. Instead it remained obdurately in my hand crinkling and bubbling. Finally a few butterflies of flame crept up the glossy paper and devoured the man's socks.

I tried again and, after several minutes, flames destroyed everything except two sets of genitalia. I tossed these down the toilet and pulled the chain; water churned, the cistern gargled but the charred organs remained jauntily bobbing on the water.

When they finally disappeared I still had five more pictures to destroy. Desperately I tried to set fire to another picture, this time of the man clutching his piece apparently unsure where to put it.

Again after an indecent interval the flames destroyed everything except private parts, and it occurred to me how bizarre it would be if the KGB burst in now and caught me brandishing this burnt offering. An unparalleled example of English sexual eccentricity.

Sweating and mumbling, I made a pyre of the remaining photographs in the bath and threw match after match into

15

their midst until all that remained of their dispirited coupling was a heap of black ashes. As the last flame died I heard a thunderous knocking on the door of the apartment. I grabbed the ashes, dropped them in the pan and pulled the chain.

I opened the door expecting to be marched off to Lubyanka Prison for interrogation on the latest Anglo-Saxon trends in perversion. Robin Stafford stood there, large and amiable and reassuring; he had forgotten his key.

He told me later over a Scotch that the photographs had been in the apartment when he took over. He had forgotten them. "Did you get that, Fred?" he asked the light-fitting.

II

My mood next morning was exuberant, apprehension of the previous evening remote and farcical.

The sky was metallic blue; frost sparkled on the rooftops and far below traffic crawled along the wide expanses of Kutuzovsky Prospect as though pulled by threads. Across the avenue stood the gloriously vulgar hulk of the Ukraina Hotel.

I was in the most awesome and blinkered capital city of the most powerful — or second most powerful, according to the way you looked at it — country in the world. The prospects were daunting but I was determined to peer behind the conventional pictures painted by both Western and Soviet propagandists and, at the same time, enjoy myself.

While Robin took a bath, I boiled an egg beside the congealed borsch, brewed myself a pot of tea and adjourned to the lounge-cum-dining-room, a bright but cavernous place appointed with bruised furniture, an ancient record-player, brass candlesticks and a bar which was the focal point.

I was half way through my egg when the staff of two arrived. First Valentina, massively built with bright red hair, an ear-to-ear grin and an appetite that could empty a larder for a mid-morning snack. She looked like a Russian doll and, when pleased by a comment about her cooking, administered bone-cracking hugs that wouldn't have disgraced a Saturday-afternoon wrestler.

17

Valentina was closely followed by Dima, the interpreter, a gentle, bespectacled young man whose duties forced him, with considerable dismay, to straddle the worlds of Marxist-Leninism and Western bourgeois decadence.

Introductions were carried out by Robin who emerged damply but majestically from the bathroom wearing a blue and white-spotted, silk dressing-gown.

Both Dima and Valentina had for years looked after a succession of *Expressmen* and they were both anxious to test the mettle of the new recruit. Valentina more than Dima, because she was concerned whether her reign in the kitchen was to continue.

Dima, who spoke better English than I did, translated for Valentina and myself. "Did Gaspadeen Lambert enjoy the borsch which I left on the stove?"

"Absolutely delicious," I replied.

Dima, as honest a man as you could find within the system, smiled grimly. Like Robin he knew that the borsch had been bubbling on the stove for as long as the sugar-coated red-currant had been under the television set.

"Would Gaspadeen Lambert like a cup of tea?" Obviously a well-tried restorative for correspondents with skulls full of last night's vodka fumes.

"Very much. Milk with no sugar, please."

And then, with a coy giggle: "Is that how Gaspadeen Lambert's wife likes her tea?"

A long pause. Dima polished his spectacles; a great polisher of lenses was Dima. For me the innocent-sounding question posed problems. My marriage had broken up, a casualty of my profession and certainly no fault of my wife's; subsequently I had fallen in love with a green-eyed French-Canadian air stewardess and hoped to get her established in Moscow.

Breathing heavily, Valentina stared expectantly at me; Dima gave his spectacles another perfectionist's polish; Robin hummed a few bars of no known melody.

Finally, giving nothing away, I told her through Dima; "Diane likes one lump of sugar." No deception there: Diane did like one lump, although she wasn't my wife.

"Ah." It was only later I realised that they were both perfectly well aware of my situation. Like all staff allotted to foreigners they were employed by the UPKD, a Government department that collaborated with the secret police — and there was little doubt that the KGB were well briefed on my mating habits. What Valentina really wanted to know was whether a mistress was to be infiltrated into her domain.

Valentina was plainly far from satisfied by my answer and followed up with a supplementary question which Dima ignored; if he was ever guilty of deceit I like to think that it was through omission rather than fabrication.

Smiling uncertainly, Valentina retired to her primitive kitchen to re-activate the borsch, in repose as black as printers' ink, brew the tea and prepare her first snack of the day. And Dima retreated into the office to paste up Robin's latest cuttings from the *Express*.

In the lounge Robin confided that Dima was the best interpreter assigned to any foreign journalist, unswervingly loyal to both Kremlin and correspondent. A daunting task that would have split the personality of a lesser man.

But I often wondered what turned over in his mind as he compared the turgid doctrinaire of *Pravda* or *Izvestia* with the breezy articles in the *Express* that savaged British policies as scathingly as Russian. No matter, he knew where to find the important stories in *Pravda* — on the back page in small print.

If Dima had one weakness it was the Abominable Snowman. The big hairy creature was the passion of his life. He possessed most known works on the subject and had taken a holiday in Georgia in the hope that the Yeti, sensing the presence of a devoted admirer, would leap from the forest and

19

extend a hirsute paw. No such luck; but Dima was undeterred. Whenever he managed to manoeuvre the conversation round to the beast, his eyes gleamed fanatically behind his gold-rimmed spectacles and it was inadvisable to question its existence.

Because of their personalities Valentina and Dima were already destroying some of the misconceptions about Russia on which I had been fed for so long; namely, that all gaiety was extinguished after the Revolution and the Soviet people were moulded from grey plasticine. Soviet notions about the West are, of course, equally hare-brained. London is still believed to be a Dickensian stew seething around oases of privilege. And the culprits in both cases are creaking old publicity machines — Caxton printing presses in the age of the computer.

Not that I harboured any illusions about the Soviet regime: Fred, connected clandestinely to the light-fitting, provided the proof that I had arrived in a land governed by fear. But perhaps the people were not uniformly drab, wearing coat-hangers inside their suits and wintry scowls on their faces . . .

While a workman from the UPKD stuck strips of paper around the windows to keep out the gathering cold, Robin took me into the office to explain the daily routine.

With a considerable time difference in force between Moscow and London we possessed the inestimable advantage that we didn't have to telephone the foreign desk until midday, when those faraway deskmen were just getting to grips with the globe. By that time an item for their daily schedule — that hallowed document without which a deskman is as helpless as a lawyer without a brief — could be found: an attack on drunkenness in *Pravda*, a visit from some tame, visiting politician, a space shot, a Red Square rally . . .

Unless an exceptional story was breaking, the 'phone call was followed by gargantuan lunches served by Valentina; a Press briefing, perhaps, given by a British Embassy official —

a chummy gathering memorable only for its futility; the dictation of a story to London; a couple of cocktail parties where it was possible to pick up the occasional story from a liquor-liberated diplomat; adjournment to the British Club where you could drink a pint of bitter and watch a *Carry On* movie.

Today Dima had already cut out a few possible stories from the Soviet Press and the reams of teletype torn off the Tass machine. Robin picked out an item about 'hooligan behaviour' on a collective farm and telephoned London.

Contacting the office was never difficult. The *Express* always put in floating calls to Moscow, a system by which you picked up a call instead of putting one in. These floaters were made using an agreed pseudonym; thus if there was a call for a Gaspadeen Bollinger you could take it or leave it; but if there was a call for Gaspadeen Lambert then, by God, they wanted you.

Having told the *Express* switchboard what the weather was like in Moscow, a hurdle that always had to be vaulted, Robin spoke to David English, then handed me the receiver.

English's breezy tones evoked a vision of the *Express* editorial floor, a sprawling arena of green-topped desks chattering with noisy endeavour channelled towards the daily miracle, the first edition. Momentarily the vision was unattainably cosy, like a lighted parlour viewed from a blizzard. I saw a tall, gangling reporter arrive at the first desk on the left and bury his head in the first mug of tea of the day. Me!

"Are you there, old boy?"

Yes, I said, I was there.

"Settling in all right?"

"Fine, just fine," if you discounted burning dirty pictures in the bog.

"Great. Well, you're in luck. We've got a good story for you." His enthusiasm was as infectious as always.

I waited expectantly; the possibilities were limitless — a

21

Kremlin intrigue, an interview with Philby or Maclean, a Chinese incursion into Soviet territory . . .

"Desmond Morris is flying out."

Desmond *Who*? (This was long before he had won fame as the author of *The Naked Ape*.)

"You know, the chap from London Zoo. He's flying out to superintend Chi Chi and An An . . ."

Which was how I learned that, far from being plunged into some perilous baptisimal, I was to spend the next few days in Moscow Zoo waiting for two giant pandas to mate.

Was sex totally inescapable in Moscow?

*   *   *

The panda stint, however, didn't start immediately and for a few days, escorted by Robin, I tried to preserve my first impressions of the city like pressed flowers in an album.

The advance scouts of winter — a few flakes of snow peeling from the sky, bruised clouds assembling on the horizon, the first frosted breaths from Siberia, the golden cupolas of the Kremlin riding high above it all, majestic but frail in the occasional autumn sunshine.

Narrow streets in which I wandered, lost, among the broad highways; here and there wooden houses with fretted eaves, crumbs of the past left among the rearing cubes of the present.

Gorky Park with its mossy lakes and bands of youths strumming farewell to summer on their guitars; the subway, buried beneath all seasons, each station a burnished monument to achievement or endeavour — and an indelible reproof to the subway systems of New York and London.

Black Zil and Chaika limousines, provided for Kremlin VIP's swanning along centre traffic lanes reserved for them — my second realisation that in a Communist society privilege is more arrogantly exhibited than in a democracy.

22

Red Square, its cobbles polished by marching feet, and the gaudy baubles of St Basil's Cathedral; the queue outside Lenin's Tomb shuffling forward in perpetual motion.

Ice-cream vendors, mini-tankers delivering *kvas*, a beverage that tastes like sour tea; kiosks selling sweets and propaganda and paper-thin postcards.

And everywhere the city closing up like a sea anenome that suddenly senses danger. Out came the fur hats, coats as heavy as carpets, *valenki* boots fashioned from felt. Into car radiators went vodka, more reliable than Soviet anti-freeze; snow-ploughs and old ladies with shovels stood by . . .

I visited GUM, the department store that looked like a church bazaar in a cathedral, the Bolshoi Ballet where, between acts, I drank pink champagne with a maraschino cherry bobbing on the bubbles, a church preserved like a museum piece as proof of a liberal attitude towards religion, and all the monuments to heroism.

But all of these have been exhaustively described. As have the statistics of a nation embracing fifteen republics, one hundred tongues, eleven time zones and 262.4 million people occupying nearly one-seventh of the world's land surface; the attitude of Authority towards pop music and modern art; the handful of intellectuals baying their defiance; and so on.

What has always been difficult to find is something new to write about this vast land, to escape from the official catalogue. I decided that in this book a light-hearted approach might open a few slats of light; but, despite the irreverent intent, it is impossible to be completely non-political about a people who are fed party dogma from the teat to the paps of old-age.

What angered me then, as now, was the expenditure on military strength and expansionism — even to the stars — at the expense of the living standards of those people. That and the abject attitude of visiting left-wingers from other countries, blindly determined to see their principles triumphing.

Communism, with its emotive appeal of equality, has had all the chances of the favourite in a one-horse race to triumph; but it has failed as these visitors would have realised had they removed their blinkers and assessed queues, the shortages, overcrowding and, above all, loss of liberty.

Such guests were, of course, given the treatment. Ivan Ivanovich and his devoted family living in a model apartment; shops stacked with luxury goods (available only to the privileged); tame factory workers expressing joy that they had exceeded their quota. Everywhere heroic achievement — washed down with champagne and vodka.

And back home strutted the poor, stage-managed puppets, to trumpet the glories of practical Communism!

* * *

Sometimes in the evenings I walked the streets of Moscow.

Some people rhapsodise about dawn. The first rays of the sun warming the night-cold earth, the smell of freshly-baked bread, birdsong, hope and promise. I have nothing against dawns: it is simply that I prefer dusk. Dusk is a time for homecoming. Lighted windows beckon, mist dresses and soothes the day's wounds, the stars glimmer comfortingly from infinity.

Moscow in the evening betrayed its iron image. Its lights were stretched like silk on the river; old ladies appeared in the lamplight, moths seeking a flame; liquid green sparks dripped from welders on building sites and above the city, airliners from far away acknowledged home with a wink of their lights.

For me it was a gentle, evocative time when the past shared the frame of the city like a double exposure. When I was a National Serviceman the deserted Sunday night streets of Liverpool, cosy security glimpsed behind sitting-room curtains; later as a correspondent the flaring naphthalene torches of the Calcutta markets, the wet shining streets of Paris, the Sabbath calm of Tel Aviv, the whispered intrigues of Beirut.

Not that I stayed out late on those first sorties in Moscow. Because there comes a time in any evening when it turns on you, when the blade of the night is suddenly unsheathed. When this happened I turned and, as the red stars above the Kremlin came alight, scurried home pursued by the hostile darkness.

*   *   *

During this period of appraisal I was also doing the official rounds: listening while bureaucrats lectured me about the 'hooligan irresponsibility' of some foreign correspondents; returning their firm handshakes as they confided that they felt I was going to be different; loitering in the bank used by foreigners while Dima opened up an account for me, stunned by the infectious inertia of the staff.

This monthly pilgrimage to the bank was always a worrying time for Dima because both he and Valentina were paid from the money the *Express* paid into the account. If the cash failed to materialise then God help the Save the Yeti Fund.

The bulk of their salaries was paid in roubles, a percentage in dollar coupons which could be spent at the *beryozka* shops where foreigners, Kremlin officials, footballers, writers, doctors and selected defectors could buy luxury goods. Understandably the coupons were more popular.

I also met some of the other foreign correspondents. At the American Club, on the other side of the city, where you could dance with a secretary or a nanny, watch a movie and drink; or at the British Club which was mercifully on the ground floor of the complex in Kutuzovsky Prospect.

After my first game of darts at the British Club with Lenny, the British Ambassador's butler, I met Gilbert Lewthwaite of

25

the *Daily Mail*, a relative newcomer to Moscow and a cheerful, no-nonsense North Countryman determined not to be over-awed by the environment, and John Miller of the *Daily Tele-graph*, probably the best informed British correspondent in Moscow.

But we were, to an extent, in different camps. I hadn't at the time appreciated the Balkanisation of Western correspondents and I detected a certain wariness in their welcome. What transpired was that, living in other complexes, they operated within their territorial limits. Their lifeline was Reuters news agency, mine was UPI two floors above the *Express* apartment; other correspondents threw in their lot with AP.

Prominent in my camp were Lars Bringart, of the Swedish paper *Dagens Nyheter*, a cuddly but astute reporter who suc-cessfully transported a Russian folk song to Stockholm and established it in the hit parade, and Peter Worthington, a crew-cut Canadian with shrewd, Red Indian features who would stalk the streets of Moscow in sub-zero temperatures wearing only a sports-shirt. He subsequently gained fame (notoriety in the Soviet Union) by helping his female interpre-ter to defect to the West.

In the evenings Peter, who worked for a Toronto daily paper, Lars and myself would meet at the bar in the *Express* apartment, play bad chess, address the occasional remark to the light-fitting and drink whisky which, like diplomats, we could buy for about one pound a bottle.

The bar was known as the Chi Chi because the wall behind it was covered by an enormous photograph of one of the pandas who were suddenly and unexpectedly playing such a dominant role in my life. And it was at this bar, stacked with Ballantine's whisky and Stolichnaya vodka, that I first met the man who was to be my link with informative authority. His name was Vladimir, and Robin introduced him as though he were the Messiah.

He was bulkily-built but as stealthily graceful as the hunter that he was. His features were flat, his black hair sleek and thinning. He dressed well in imported mohair suits and his rumbling laugh was born deep in his barrel chest. A sophisticated Russian bear.

Vladimir was employed by the Novosti Press Agency and therefore by the KGB. When he arrived Dima vanished into the office, Robin refrained from addressing any remarks to Fred and Valentina steamed with culinary endeavour.

It was the custom of Vladimir and the resident *Expressman* to meet once a week to exchange views. One week at the *Express* apartment, the next at a Georgian restaurant where the speciality was a variety of cooked grass that tasted like spinach. At first Vladimir regaled me with jokes, part of the recognised exchange with Robin who could certainly tell a tale. I couldn't; nor was I a good listener, waiting, sweaty-palmed for the punch-line, and irritating the raconteur by tittering prematurely. But Vladimir soon realised this — it doesn't take long — and adapted: instead of joke-telling sessions we used to have impassioned arguments about blood sports.

Much of our passion stemmed from the amount of liquor consumed. Vladimir had a prodigious capacity but with my Fleet Street training behind me, I could also sink a few. The result was that, before and over lunch, we killed a bottle of vodka — Stolichnaya chilled in the deep freeze until it poured slurred from the bottle, as thick as oil — and a bottle of Georgian wine accompanied by Narzan mineral water, followed by a few drams of brandy.

If we had any secret gems of information to exchange then they were soon forgotten, and after we had parted, growling throatily about the rights and wrongs of bull-fighting, I fell purple-faced into bed and oblivion. If ever there was a man with whom I should like to have forged a life-long friendship it was Vladimir; but we were helpless on different sides of the

27

tracks, and all we could do was brush hands and await the inevitable parting.

On the first meeting, however, the friendship was almost still-born. Robin had introduced us, a few jokes had been told, the conversation had progressed onto materialistic possessions — cars, radios and cameras.

I stole away to my bedroom, returning with a new Pentax camera that I had bought in London. Vladimir examined it politely and returned it to me. Then I aimed the camera at the two of them, suggesting a farewell photograph for their albums. Vladimir frowned into his drink, even Robin's composure faltered.

"Come on," I urged like a pestilent street photographer, "just one."

"I don't think so," Robin said stiffly. "Some other time . . ."

"But there won't be another time."

At this moment Vladimir broke free and headed for the bathroom. While he was away Robin, striving to keep tight control over himself, told me that Russians were averse to having their photographs taken, especially KGB Russians who presumed that copies of the photograph would immediately be transmitted to the CIA and MI6.

"For your own sake," Robin breathed heavily, "I wouldn't try it again."

The atmosphere over lunch was strained. Perhaps, I thought, I should put the camera on the floor and jump on it. But finally the frigidity broke up in a series of boisterous toasts.

But both Vladimir and I had learned our respective lessons. No jokes, no photographs. And on that tacit understanding, our microcosm of Anglo-Soviet friendship prospered.

Soon after that I adjourned to the Moscow Zoo. In fact I spent my thirty-seventh birthday there, silently imploring Chi Chi, the big black-and-white bear brought from London, to allow An An, the Russian panda, to mount her. The object of the exercise, stage-managed by Dr Morris, Curator of Mammals at London Zoo and Dr Igor Sosnovsky, his Soviet counterpart, was to produce the first baby panda born in captivity.

Not if Chi Chi was having anything to do with it, it wasn't.

The zoologists put the two great beasts together and nothing happened; they separated them — in case absence made the heart grow fonder — and nothing happened when they were reunited; disconcertingly they then discovered that Chi Chi, a sort of Greta Garbo of the ursine world, preferred their company to An An's.

The temperature had by now fallen to minus three degrees centigrade; when it did struggle above freezing point it rained. I camped miserably around the cage, brooding on Desmond Morris' match-making enthusiasms and the circumstances that had combined to deposit me not just in Moscow but in surroundings I had always detested — a zoological gardens.

'Gardens' is, of course, a deliberate misnomer. Zoos are prisons. Fatuously, zoologists still maintain the pretence that animals revel in captivity. They must surely avert their eyes, and their consciences, when they pass the cages where the lions, born to roam the sun-baked bush beneath high blue skies, plod back and forth as ceaselessly as the waves. Whenever I reluctantly visit a zoo, I like to believe that it is the humans who are being paraded for the delectation of the animals.

Moscow Zoo wasn't much different from any other zoo, except that it seemed to be blessedly free of stick-poking, bun-throwing spectators: the public obeyed the warning notices and that, perhaps, was something in favour of the authority of a totalitarian state.

Finally, on October 14, 1966 on page two — the main

29

foreign page which carried the strapline DIALLING THE WORLD — I recorded the momentous news that the zoologists had decided to abandon their efforts to persuade Chi Chi to take a Russian lover.

After that I would, I thought, be able to settle down to some serious reporting about Mother Russia and her people. But such grandiose aspirations were soon dispelled. My next assignment was reporting the arrival of Hughie Green and his television quiz show *Double Your Money* in Moscow.

Two shows were pre-recorded for screening in Britain. In Russia the programme was called *Do You Want To Go On?* because it was deemed to be undignified to compete for money — but not for cameras or television sets.

All went well in the warm-up session until Hughie Green said: "Now is the time for anyone sitting with anyone else's wife to move."

There was an uneasy silence. The usually exuberant Mr Green looked puzzled. Finally a voice from the audience announced: "There is no-one married here."

III

Work apart, my first priority was to get Diane to Russia. She had resigned from East African Airways and, having bought a cheap air ticket to Moscow — the last concession of her job — was awaiting my summons at her parents' home in Montreal.

Her father, who had been a diplomat in Rome and Paris, was solicitous but pessimistic about our future, taking the view that as soon as she arrived in Moscow we would both be compromised and subsequently blackmailed or dispatched to a labour camp.

But, as the weeks passed and autumn started to freeze into winter, it began to look as though his worries were groundless because the Soviet Consulate in Ottawa refused to grant Diane a visa.

She telephoned twice a week to report the latest frustration and, while I took the call in the office, Lars Bringart and Peter Worthington waited expectantly in the Chi Chi bar.

"Well?" they demanded in unison when I returned, because they were becoming heartily sick of this gloomy, love-sick fellow who had replaced the ebullient Robin. (After ten days of kindly and meticulous tutorship he had finally departed for Rome.)

A ponderous shake of the head. "The poor little thing's been told to try again next week."

After a month of this depressing dialogue they referred to her as 'the little thing'.

"Any news of the little thing?"

A sigh of deep melancholia.

"Poor little thing," as they returned to their chess and remembered sparkling evenings with Robin regaling them with anecdotes.

The agony of these 'phone-calls was compounded by a trans-Atlantic echo. The result was that I had to listen to a repetition of whatever idiocy I had uttered before I could hear Diane. If it was particularly inane then I tried to correct it — and had to listen to the correction. Meanwhile Diane would reply while I was still listening to my own voice.

Thus a touch of farce, unappreciated by the protagonists, entered our conversations with exchanges such as:

"Daily Express here . . . Express here . . ."

". . . Derek."

"I didn't catch that . . . didn't catch that . . ."

". . . catch what?"

"What you said . . . you said . . ."

". . . love you."

Did love me or didn't love me?

"Say that again . . . that again . . ."

". . . drunk?"

"No, not drunk . . . not drunk . . ."

The nadir of these emotionally exhausting conversations was reached one evening when Diane called and announced: "It's hopeless."

The Russian Consul, I gathered, had finally told her that it was difficult enough for a wife to obtain a visa; to issue one to a mistress was out of the question and she might as well forget the whole thing.

Although Diane is petite and exudes femininity, she approaches any challenge with a formidable singleness of purpose. If she said the situation was hopeless then there was no hope.

Peter and Lars gazed apprehensively at my despairing figure as I lurched out of the office and tossed back a vodka, groaning melodramatically as it hit my stomach. When I had explained what had happened, Lars, benign and bespectacled, put his arm round my bowed shoulders and, ever inventive, said: "Let's go out and get drunk."

Even though he wasn't a great drinker, Peter, honed features grim beneath his crew-cut, agreed out of desperation; in fact he was so dismayed by the humourless future stretching ahead that he actually put on a jacket before going out into the cold.

We drove in Peter's Mercedes to the National Hotel, like the Metropole a stately relic of Czarist days. Provided you ate in the hard-currency restaurant reserved for foreigners and VIP's, you could dine relatively well, especially if you chose the julienne which was served, thick and spicy, in small earthenware bowls.

Unfortunately, such was the doom-laden mood of the evening, I chose steak. Calculating that this would take an hour to prepare we ordered a couple of bottles of Russian champagne. Gradually my Chekhovian despair turned to anger.

Observing this, Peter, his voice as soft as his physical appearance was hard, said: "You've got to get tough with the bastards, you know."

"He's right," agreed Lars, who enjoyed a punch-up as much as the next man, although his verbal sparring in English was sabotaged by his inability to pronounce H's. "You've got to give them gell," he added helpfully.

Determined not to be intimidated by anyone, we ordered another bottle of champagne, the bubbles bursting in our glasses like explosions of protest. The meal ultimately arrived. Their bowls of julienne smelled delicious, but my steak looked

33

like an elephant dropping. It was also cold and impervious to any assault with knife and fork.

My depression and anger crystallised into an insane hatred of the black cannonball on my plate. I picked it up and hurled at the retreating back of the waiter. With a sixth sense alerted by life in a police state, he ducked — and the steak landed on a table occupied by four West German diplomats.

"God help us," muttered Lars.

Expressionless, the waiter retrieved the steak and replaced it on my plate, while the rest of the diners observed the scene with puzzled interest, like an audience who has missed the first reel of a movie.

The waiter murmured a few words in Russian and returned to the kitchens. According to Lars he said, "I believe you dropped this sir."

Unrepentant, but prepared to be expelled, justifiably, from Russia, I returned to Kutuzovsky Prospect with Peter and Lars. Next morning my fury was unabated. *"You've got to get tough with the bastards!"*

Vladimir was on holiday and his place at the fortnightly luncheon at the apartment had been taken by another KGB agent, balding with a beaky face and a wary manner.

The incident at the National wasn't mentioned; instead my guest confined himself to asking questions about my first impressions of Moscow.

"Bloody awful," I told him.

He looked perturbed. Why, he asked, did I feel that way. Hadn't everything been done to make me feel at home?

Not quite everything . . . Articulately and vehemently I told him that I would never be able to enjoy anything the Soviet Union had to offer while a beautiful, green-eyed air stewardess languished in Montreal. More to the point, I seriously doubted whether I should ever be able to write anything favourable about a regime so deafened by the grinding wheels of bureaucracy that it couldn't hear the beating of two lovers' hearts.

The lyricism seemed to stun him. After a moment's pause he said: "May I use your telephone?"

Five minutes later he returned from the office, sat down, raised his glass of Georgian wine and said: "Here's to love."

"But not mine," I remarked, clinking glasses.

He put down his glass, tapped the side of his formidable nose and said: "You will be speaking to Diane" — I hadn't even mentioned her name — "some time this evening?"

"It's possible," I said.

"Tell her to return to the consulate in Ottawa tomorrow."

She did — and was immediately handed a visa by the consul who was as dumbfounded as she was.

*   *   *

Such crises of travel and communication shouldn't have surprised either of us: we had been beset by them since we first met in Salisbury in the autumn of 1965.

Often I would arrive in some sweltering African city to cover a story at the same moment as she, as an air stewardess, was due to depart to the town I had just left. It was because of these frustrations that I was once guilty of dereliction of duty.

Diane had just arrived in Nairobi from London; I had just arrived there from Salisbury. In euphoric mood we adjourned to the Norfolk Hotel — and found a cable instructing me to fly Air Congo to Leopoldville to pick up a connection there to Nigeria where there had been a revolution.

The prospects were depressing. The likelihood of an Air Congo aircraft ever reaching its destination was debatable; the possibility of making a connection to anywhere farther away than the end of the runway remote.

I sent a telex to the office pointing this out and suggesting

35

that a Pan Am flight from Nairobi to West Africa the follow-ing day was preferable. That, I added to clinch my case, was the way Peter Younghusband of the *Daily Mail* — gigantic of stature and unbeatable at communications — intended to travel.

Back came the merciless reply: FLY AIR CONGO AS INSTRUCTED.

Morosely we took a taxi to Nairobi's Embakasi Airport, hoping that the Air Congo pilot had landed in the game park. But there was the aircraft, looking as though it was waiting for Baron von Richthofen to do battle with a squadron of Sopwith Camels.

When I reached the ticket counter I discovered to my joy that I had left my Air Travel card behind at the hotel. Gleefully I told a taciturn Air Congo clerk the bad news. No trouble, he said, they would hold the plane until I had retrieved the credit card from the hotel.

One hour later, accompanied by three other passengers resentful at the delay, I took off and headed west. The cabin was insufferably hot; blades of sunlight glinted on the wings; the engines spluttered in protest at the whole aeronautical exercise. And all the time, as we lumbered over the bush far below, I was heading away from Diane.

The first stop was Entebbe and it was there that I had the glimmering of a plan. Dereliction it certainly was; on the other hand I was still convinced that the Pan Am flight from Nairobi was the best means of reaching Nigeria.

From Entebbe airport I telephoned the *Express'* Uganda correspondent and told him to contact London and tell them that I was suffering from a severe attack of dysentery.

On we flew across territory that, from the air, looked like fields of broccoli, until we landed in a series of longhops at Bujumbura, capital of Burundi.

There on the tarmac was an East African Fokker Friendship

waiting to take off for Nairobi. Hysterically I told the Air Congo stewardess to get someone to unload my luggage and transfer it to the Nairobi-bound plane.

Accustomed to white men affected by the heat, she said, "But you have just come from Nairobi," standing in front of me, arms akimbo, ready to apply emergency measures if I became violent.

"I know I've just come from Nairobi," I told her. "And I want to go back."

"You got a ticket to Leopoldville and that's where you're going," she said, pushing me firmly in the chest as I tried to stand up.

An unseemly brawl between a black stewardess and a gibbering white foreign correspondent might have ensued if it had not been for the intervention of an enlightened Belgian pilot who could readily understand anyone's reluctance to visit Leopoldville

My baggage was unloaded and hurled onto the Friendship as it was about to taxi to the end of the runway. Ten minutes later I was airborne once again, retracing my journey.

At Entebbe I telephoned Diane in Nairobi, only to learn that, having put me on a plane to darkest Leopoldville, she had volunteered for a flight to New Delhi!

I shouted incoherent entreaties and imprecations into the telephone and dashed out to the Friendship watched by curious passengers who, no doubt, had expected me to hurl myself onto a Leopoldville-bound flight.

Happily Diane managed to cancel the Indian flight; we spent one night together and next day I took off once again for West Africa with Peter Younghusband on the Pan Am flight.

Ten days later, having covered the Nigerian coup, I returned to Nairobi — and was immediately taken sick with dysentery.

Diane's arrival in Moscow was equally anticlimactic. As soon as she had collected her visa in Ottawa the weather in Moscow socked down. Snow fell and melted and vaporised, shrouding the city's airports in fog.

She managed to reach Warsaw on an Air India flight, but couldn't fly any further, and our telephone calls were resumed to the dismay of Lars and Peter.

Finally she called to tell me: "I'm being thrown out of the hotel. I'll have to fly to Leningrad and catch the night train to Moscow. I have," she added seductively, "brought you a bottle of whisky."

Although I had enough Scotch in the apartment to fuel the Highland Games, I thanked her effusively and retired to bed.

Next morning the fog had lifted and sunlight gilded the rooftops. I put two bottles of champagne on ice and drove to the station trembling with anticipation. I was greeted on the platform by Diane waving the bottle of Scotch (empty). She pointed at a man with a bald head and said, "You owe Mr Baumgarten twenty pounds."

A confused tale followed. She and Baumgarten, also in transit in Warsaw, had flown together to Leningrad. There she had been installed in a sleeping compartment on the Moscow train with another girl, the remaining two bunks being piled high with instruments belonging to a travelling orchestra. However, two soldiers had subsequently demanded accommodation and the instruments had been shovelled into the corridor. At which stage in this remarkable journey the whisky had been emptied from the bottle was never explained. But as far as I could make out Baumgarten had lent Diane the twenty pounds to buy food in Leningrad.

Not quite the stuff of Barbara Cartland. But who cared? We were together.

Diane's arrival considerably enlivened the scene.

One by one the resident correspondents called at the apartment to gaze in wonderment at the girl who had been granted a visa without a marriage-line in sight, and she managed to charm such diverse characters as the British Ambassador, Sir Geoffrey Harrison, and a brooding KGB operative who brought her presents from the *Beryozka* shop and wept while he recited Russian poetry to her.

She began to teach French to Dima — stumbling a little over Abominable Snowman — and persuaded Valentina to pour the saucepan of borsch down the sink. Peter and Lars were captivated both by her green-eyed, elfin looks and her ability to spit a jet of beer ten feet through the air.

The condition of the apartment appalled her and she gave it an autumn-clean, finding, among other articles, a pair of Marks and Spencer's knickers in the office files on Russian Cultural Life. The sugar-coated red-currant, she agreed, should stay under the television.

But her supreme achievement was to master a decent amount of Russian within a few weeks. Armed with this she stormed Moscow's stores haggling enthusiastically with muscular female assistants. Confronted by this petite dynamo mouthing torrents of broken Russian, the women mostly gave up, and good-humouredly handed over the goods.

She threw parties, she cooked when borsch and Chicken Kiev had begun to pall, she dressed exquisitely as French-Canadian girls usually can — and she succeeded in outraging the matrons of one particular Moscow suburb and one of the more introverted members of the British Embassy staff.

The cause of the outrage in the suburbs was a mini-skirt. It would be an original newspaper feature, I decided, to observe the reactions of Muscovite women to a decadent Western temptress wearing a skirt half way up her thighs.

Diane, we agreed, should walk along a street while I lurked behind, discreetly snapping away with my camera. But we were quite unprepared for the ferocity of the women's reactions. They spat, they shouted, they clenched their fists.

Diane continued bravely on her way but I stepped in and aborted the mission before she was dismembered. In any case, was it so funny to taunt women in headscarves and inferior quality print dresses who would never have a chance to wear anything better?

The clash with the lower-echelon diplomat at the British Embassy was more rewarding. The Embassy was a baronial building, once the property of a sugar merchant, across the Moscow River from the spires and domes of the Kremlin, and life there proceeded at a stately pace except when Russians tried to seek asylum or George Brown flew in.

In his office there this particular diplomat applied himself studiously to the study of protocol and supervised invitations to Embassy functions, in particular the Christmas ball.

My invitation to the ball duly arrived, addressed only to me. As Diane was by now a familiar figure on the cocktail party circuit, I telephoned this young administrator to make sure that she, too, was invited.

"Ah," he said.

"Ah what?"

"I'm glad you telephoned," he said

"Ah."

A pause while he assembled his diplomacy. Then: "You and Miss Brunet are not . . . um, you know . . . not . . . well . . ."

"We're not married," I told him. "We're living in sin and loving every moment of it."

"Ah," he said.

"Does it matter?"

"Not to me, of course," he said.

"Who does it matter to then?"

"Well," he said, solemnly, "I'm not sure that H.E. would approve."

40

This was patently nonsense because Sir Geoffrey Harrison, elegant and silver-haired, was both the personification of a career diplomat and an enlightened aristocrat who understood the privations of his countrymen in Moscow.

"Are you saying that Diane isn't invited?"

"Well, put like that I suppose the answer must be yes."

"Then put like this," I said, "you can get stuffed."

"Oh come on there, *Express*."

"I'm not a bloody horse," I said and replaced the receiver.

We didn't attend the ball and happily our absence was noted by Sir Geoffrey who promptly invited us to lunch.

"Both of us?" I asked.

He looked surprised. "But of course. You *and* Miss Brunet."

It was a delightful lunch, both Sir Geoffrey and his wife excellent hosts. Although the dignity of the occasion did falter momentarily when, as I was bidding farewell, a butler slipped me a couple of Sir Geoffrey's cigars and hissed: "Here you are, Derek, mate, a fair old smoke these."

But the most satisfying aspect of the lunch was the knowledge that the invitations to myself *and* Miss Brunet had been issued by the same student of etiquette who had been responsible for the guest-list to the Christmas ball.

IV

Moscow was by now a steel box filled with feathers.

The cold locked roads and airports and at night bladed the skyline; but inside these confines snow fell softly and thickly and patterns of ferns and flowers grew on the windows, and the parks were filled with the cries of children and the songs of skates.

The cold also trapped camaraderie within the city so that it burned like a camp fire in a frozen desert. Muscovites herded together in bus and subway discussing the cold with their annual astonishment; they skied and skated and, with rasping shovels, cleared the streets; they visited each other's apartments, sang soulfully and drank prodigiously, queued for the Bolshoi, the circus and the cinema; they shared the cold and were joined by it.

And all the while, except for an occasional golden day or starlit night, the snow fell. Either gently, with flakes hesitating in the lamplight, or wildly, with cross-currents sweeping them across the streets to cake pedestrians into stiff-limbed marionettes, but always remorselessly so that every morning the snow-plough emerged from the wings to churn the night collection into the gutters.

Pathways in the parks were sprayed with water so that you could skate to work; old men, as hard as Siberia, brooded over out-of-door chess-boards on those occasional clear but ice-polished days, blowing jets of frosted breath over a doomed king.

In the western ghettos the cold was everything. To some it was an enemy which icily underlined their predicament — some hesitated on the brink of a mental breakdown, a few committed suicide; to others it was an ally that enhanced the snugness of indoors and drew them closer to their hosts.

Hosts such as *babushkas*, old women cocooned in furs and shawls and felt boots who would stop you in the street and point to your cheeks to warn you about frostbite; hosts such as shopkeepers melted by the warmth of their stores and taxi-drivers who sweated sullenly in the summer but enjoyed the winter-sport of their profession sliding round corners, slithering broadside down the wide avenues, spinning like tops as they braked on the ice.

One cab driver at the wheel of a black Moskvich braked, spun and, with wheels locked, crashed into the side of the Cortina.

When he climbed out of his cab, navigating the cold as though it were a wall, it was apparent that he was classically drunk. Weaving around, throwing playful punches, winking elaborately and spilling forth a torrent of words. At one point he stood in the middle of the road, kicked his cab and said: "My taxi is yours. My wife is yours. Have you got a drink?"

Sadly Dima and I surveyed the damage to the Cortina, a buckled wing and a dent in one of the front doors. Dima, forever apprehensive but nonetheless courageous, informed me: "It is illegal to drive a damaged car in Russia."

"Well, we can't leave the thing here," I told him. I gave the demented taxi-driver a friendly punch on the shoulder and drove off.

In fact I drove the damaged Cortina for another six months and was reprimanded only once by a militiaman who finally gave up, defeated by my linguistic shortcomings.

43

It was also an offence, punishable by a rouble fine on the spot, to drive a dirty car, but this was only implemented in the summer; in any case the *Express* employed a Muscovite to clean and warm up the Cortina every morning.

The cold also drew closer together my small community — Diane, Valentina, Dima and associate members, Peter Worthington, Lars Bringart and Vladimir.

In the office Dima adapted to my erratic authority, finally confessing that he hadn't always understood Stafford's jokes.

He acted as interpreter, guide, liaison officer and political tutor. Such tutorship occurred when I pointed out some particularly feeble passage of drivel in *Pravda*, *Izvestia* or *Trud*.

"How, Dima, can any intelligent person swallow anything as indigestible as this?"

"Because we are believers," he would say. "We don't have to have articles dressed and trimmed. All we need are the bare facts unlike readers of the Western Press," flourishing a copy of some decadent newspaper or other.

I admired his loyalty but viewed his opinion of British newspapers with scepticism because there was no comparison between the columns of pompous dogma in the Soviet papers and the flair and wit of their Western counterparts.

Sometimes in the afternoons, when the first calls to the office had been made and I was weighted to my chair by one of Valentina's lunches, Dima would open his files on the Abominable Snowman. And behind his gold-rimmed spectacles his gentle eyes would gleam fanatically.

So exhaustive were his files and so intense was his belief that he almost persuaded me that the creatures existed and, as snow poured past the window, we spent the darkening hours deep in discussion about hairy monsters instead of Kremlin policy.

At that hour known to the English as tea-time Dima would put on his overcoat, long woollen scarf and fur hat and depart for I knew not where. Once when the wind was knifing

44

through the city, slicing at any expanse of exposed flesh, I offered to drive him home.

He looked doubtful, but as the wind hurled snow as hard as grapeshot against the window he relented. But he was ill at ease seated in the Cortina as we drove through the winter-cruel, ice-crackling streets.

When he finally asked me to stop he didn't say he was home because that would have been a lie. Perhaps he caught a bus for the last lap of the journey. I never knew; nor did I ever know where he lived or ever meet his wife or children.

Details about Valentina's home background were equally vague although on one occasion she did drop a few hints about the state of her marriage.

Diane, exasperated by her cavalier attitude to housework, had determined to make a stand. After several false starts she finally cornered Valentina in the kitchen — no mean feat — and uttered words to the effect: "Today we have got to have this out."

The reaction to these stern words was a wondrous smile that embraced Valentina's red hair, blue eyes, gleaming white teeth and rouged cheeks. According to Diane she followed up this puzzling manifestation of contrition with the comment: "That is wonderful news."

Nonplussed, Diane retreated to her corner, poured herself a glass of wine and came back fighting. "It has been going on a long time," she said.

Valentina flung wide her arms and said: "For twenty-five glorious years."

Believing that she was drunk, Diane took more evasive action and, leaving herself space to escape down the corridor, asked: "What has been going on for twenty-five years?"

"My marriage to my wonderful husband," Valentina cried ecstatically. "We were married twenty-five years ago today." And she produced a bottle of champagne.

45

At least Diane knew when she was licked. Champagne frothed around the kitchen and, after a couple of glasses, Valentina confided that she and her husband had been parted for a couple of years when he had been fighting the Germans but, since then, they had been together and they had never quarrelled.

Mind you, it would have taken a man courageous to a fault to have risked the best of three falls with our heavy-weight treasure.

At regular intervals both she and Dima were required to report to the KGB on the behaviour and attitudes of Gaspadeen Lambert. I subsequently learned that their reports were as favourable as they could intelligently make them and I was touched.

Only once was the communal spirit of the apartment disrupted — by the cockroaches. Diane didn't take to them. So she called up the UPKD and asked them to remove them.

That ever resourceful department — the Russians, like the Spanish and Irish, are great improvisers — was momentarily nonplussed. Why should anyone want to get rid of cockroaches?

"Because they're horrible," Diane said.

"But no one's ever complained before."

"I am."

Two days later a team of men wearing white boiler suits and masks arrived carrying sinister canisters, hoses and sprays. They looked as if they had come to exterminate the occupants of the apartment block rather than a few small brown insects.

Pointing at the canisters the foreman communicated the alarming information that, if we didn't vacate the apartment for three days, we would most probably suffer the same fate as the cockroaches.

We moved into Peter Worthington's flat in the next block

46

while the exterminators went about their task. When we returned a girl from the UPKD triumphantly showed us a roachless apartment. She had also come armed with an explanation of the presence of the insects that had so clearly upset a sophisticated woman of the West.

"Of course," she said, "you will have realised how they got there."

We shook our heads.

"As is well known," a familiar preliminary to a particularly obscure revelation, "there have been Negroes living in this block. They brought them with them from Africa."

The cockroaches therefore provided me with an intriguing insight into Soviet racist bigotry, an aspect of the national character not generally appreciated by Third World countries jubilantly celebrating new links with the Kremlin.

And that was the only benefit from the exercise because, within a couple of days, the cockroaches were back again, as lively and skittish as ever.

*   *   *

It was during this period that I embarked on activities that added considerable suspense to our existence. I started to write a novel about Russia.

During my Fleet Street days I had written an autobiography about a childhood in World War II called *The Sheltered Days* which had been published by Andre Deutsch and serialised on Woman's Hour on BBC radio.

Armed with this I approached an agent, a dapper trend-setting dynamo named Desmond Elliott, and suggested that whatever lay ahead of me in Moscow might form the basis of a novel.

Desmond, also the publisher of Arlington Books, responded enthusiastically. Within a few weeks he had persuaded an American hardback publisher that he had discovered another Tolstoy and duly extracted an advance from them.

The problem now was to write my *samizdat* volume inside a nest of KGB surveillance and to correspond with Desmond without creating suspicion. Not that I intended to write a violently anti-Soviet book; in fact my aim was fictionally to try and put life in Russia in its true perspective. But the sad fact was that the Kremlin was so sensitive to criticism that any adverse comment would be regarded as a criminal offence. Foreigners had been sent to labour camps for less.

Since professionally I spent much of my time at my typewriter, I was in a position to conceal the fact that I was writing a book. And whenever I left the office I took the embryonic manuscript with me. Nevertheless its presence was an acute worry because I often left it in the car and Dima would hand it to me saying: "Derek, you have forgotten your notes."

Happily, the existence of such typewritten notes was credible because I was also preparing a series for the *Express* about the fiftieth anniversary of the Bolshevik revolution. But Dima must have wondered about the attention, beyond the call of duty, that I paid to those notes. Was it really necessary to take them into the bed?

The novel, at Diane's suggestion, was to be called *Angels in the Snow*. As a child in Canada she had played a game with such a name; you lay on your back in the snow, brushed your arms up and down from head to hip and when you stood up there was the imprint of an angel.

But what would the KGB make of a correspondence about such an ethereal subject? There was no doubt that all mail was scrutinised and this, in fact, was proved beyond all doubt in my presence.

A Novosti reporter had complained to a Canadian journalist about an anti-Soviet article the latter had written. "As is well

48

known it was a pack of lies," he remarked.

"It was pretty crude, wasn't it," the Canadian agreed.

The man from Novosti looked perplexed; foreigners normally vigorously defended their stories. "You agree with me?" he asked, frowning horrendously.

"Of course I do — with one reservation. The material you're talking about was in a letter to my mother!"

Anticipating just such surveillance I had already devised a system of coded messages with Desmond Elliott. I sent letters to a forwarding address in Torquay which were dispatched to Desmond in his Mayfair offices. The main subject of this correspondence was an Uncle Albert who lived in Brighton i.e. my manuscript.

Such was the volume of letters about the ailing uncle that the KGB must have been astonished at the concern shown by a reporter, notoriously a hard-bitten species, towards an aged relative.

"Have you heard how Uncle Albert is progressing?" Desmond would inquire. "I haven't heard from him lately."

"He's making good progress," I would reply.

"Good," he would respond, "because we've found him a berth," by which I hoped he meant he had found a publisher, whereas the KGB scrutineer presumably imagined that the frail old gentleman would shortly be boarding a liner for a recuperative cruise to the West Indies.

*　　*　　*

As winter froze my initial unease melted away and life in Moscow began to seem almost more secure than it had been in London. It was, I suppose, the routine — the wary Press briefings, the cocktail parties, lunches with Vladimir, nocturnal exchanges with Fred, routine appeals for the release of Gerald Brooke, a British lecturer serving five years in a labour camp for 'subversion', regular assaults on Soviet dignity by the Chinese.

It was the Chinese, in fact, who provided me with my first serious story — the expulsion by the Russians of Red Guard students — and it was they who were responsible for plucking me from my too-cosy routine and dispatching me across Siberia.

China had recently exploded her fourth nuclear bomb and was massing troops on the disputed Sino-Soviet border in the east, some of whom had reportedly bared their backsides to the Russians across the frozen Amur River.

One evening as Diane, Lars, Peter and I were settling down to chess, the 'phone rang and David English said: "We want you to go to Siberia, old man," as though it were at the end of the Old Kent Road.

"Right oh," I said, returning to the Chi Chi bar and, with theatrical nonchalance, informing the chess-players where I was going.

The news excited Dima immensely, not because of the distance or the danger involved but because he hoped he would sight his hairy old gentleman over there. Immediately he set about the bureaucratic processes of obtaining papers for the journey. According to the pundits this would take weeks. It took one day and on the evening of the second of December we drove to Domodyedove, the domestic airport, to await our flight.

It was at Domodyedove that I discovered that there is a considerable difference between Aeroflot's domestic and international services. Unlike Sheremetyevo, this airport looked like a factory warehouse during a lunch-break. Passengers slumped in ramshackle seats looking as though they had been left over from summer; airline officials had already hibernated.

As one plump woman in a stained uniform passed by trailing yards of grey scarf I nudged Dima and said: "Who on earth do you think she is?"

Dima glanced up from one of his Yeti books and said briefly: "She's an air-stewardess."

Finally we boarded the elephantine TU-114 airliner to find that, as usual, the flight had been overbooked and two disgruntled Russians had to be ejected to make way for the Western Imperialist and his interpreter.

Then we were airborne. The airliner was sparsely furnished, the cabin service nowhere in evidence. I settled down to read an English newspaper and find out how my colleagues were reporting the close of what had been an eventful year. The Russians had made a soft landing on the moon, the Labour Party had won the General Election with an overall majority of 97, England's football team had won the World Cup — and now, I read, Harold Wilson, and Rhodesia's Ian Smith were meeting on HMS Tiger at Gibraltar to try and reach agreement over UDI.

The aircraft droned noisily eastwards and I fell asleep. At 2 a.m. I was woken by a hand shaking my shoulder while a dented tin tray was thrust under my face.

"What the hell's that?"

"Eat," said a voice.

I looked up, meeting the eyes of the plump stewardess who was now wearing her scarf tucked inside her stained jacket.

"I'm not hungry."

"Eat."

"You'd better take it from her," Dima said, sitting up and polishing his spectacles.

On the tray was a glass of mineral water, a portion of soused herring and a slice of black bread.

The stewardess stood over me, hands on her hips. "You like?"

"Smashing," I said.

51

"Smashing? What is this smashing?"

"Good," I said making smacking noises with my lips and rubbing my stomach.

"You'd better eat it," Dima said.

"I can't."

"She'll say it's criminal waste if you don't."

I picked at the raw fish, nibbled the bread, sipped the water. The stewardess stood resolutely beside me.

"You like?"

More lip-smacking.

"You eat much slowly."

I was, I agreed, a slow eater.

"Distract her," I whispered to Dima.

"I don't understand."

"Do anything. Sing, throw a fit, kiss her . . ."

This last suggestion so horrified Dima that he began to choke on his fish. While the stewardess's attention was thus distracted, I slipped my bread and fish into the pouch at the back of the seat in front of me.

When Dima had recovered from his paroxysm the stewardess looked at my empty tray suspiciously. "You say you eat much slowly," she said.

"It was so good," I said, "that I just had to gulp it down."

When Dima translated she suddenly smiled. "Is good," she said, giving me a playful punch on the shoulder. "Is good you like."

She disappeared and reappeared a couple of minutes later with another portion of raw fish, black bread and mineral water.

We arrived at Khabarovsk, half way round the world from London, at dawn and were installed in a hotel like a seaside boarding house, an incongruous establishment because Khabarovsk was a raw new city, square and sturdy and vital, a truculent intruder in the skeletal forests of the taiga. With its foundations rooted firmly in the perma frost and its sharp-cornered cubes cutting the blue sky, it was a typical pioneering post of the sixties. From such cities the Russians were journeying into the wastes to harvest energy, minerals, oil, diamonds. No longer could Siberia be dismissed as a wilderness of salt mines and prison camps. First the Trans-Siberian Railway and now the long-haul jets had changed all that.

The air glittered with the cold but there was no snow. Eagles swooped in the high blue sky; knee-booted soldiers swaggered the streets; long-haired tigers prowled the taiga. It was a place for fighters: Siberians fought the cold, the frozen earth, the tigers. Would they soon be fighting the Chinese? Most Russians shrugged away the question. They might. If they did they would win.

On our first night Dima and I adjourned to a tavern crammed with soldiers and girls with candy-floss blonde hair jiving to music played by a demented jazz group dressed like impoverished waiters at a bankrupt hotel. When the pianist crashed his fingers on the yellow fangs of the piano, sweat jumped from his forehead. The violinist was trying to saw his instrument in half; the drummer lashed his cymbals like a jockey whipping home the favourite.

I ordered two beers and, recklessly, a carafe of vodka. While we watched the piston-armed soldiers spinning their girls, we planned our respective campaigns: I intended to reach the Chinese border, Dima hoped to extend the hand of friendship to the *AS*.

But it wasn't the time or the place for such ice-cold calculations. Jackboots stomped, bouffant hair collapsed.

We downed our vodka and ordered more. You are only allowed a certain amount but here in the Wild East it didn't seem to matter. Another carafe appeared accompanied by black bread, gherkins and slices of hard white cheese.

"*Nasdarovya*," I shouted to Dima.

"Chin-chin," he responded, polishing his spectacles.

As the band mounted an assault on *Mack the Knife*, a blonde asked me to dance. Consigning everything I had read about the reserve of the Russians to the bottom of the vodka carafe, I stood up and offered her my hand.

I was promptly jerked across the floor. "Whoopee," shouted my partner, skirt spinning high above pink panties. "Beat me daddy eight to the bar."

I had never mastered the rhythms of jiving; but tonight it didn't seem to matter. The Red Army and their birds and I were as one, gyrating, sweating, chanting wild mating calls.

After the musicians had sheathed Mack and his knife and, pale and exhausted, were pouring beer down their throats, the blonde led me to a table occupied by more blonde girls and crop-haired soldiers with fierce faces. She pushed me into a chair, poured me a vodka, tossed one back herself. "You American?" she asked.

"No, English."

"We like Winston Churchill," she said.

I refrained from observing that, by all accounts, the feeling hadn't been reciprocated.

One of the soldiers with diamond blue eyes asked: "You like it here?"

"Fabulous," I answered truthfully.

"That's because we're Siberians. We do as we please."

"But you're Russians as well, aren't you?"

"Poof," said the girl. "We are Siberians."

The soldier asked: "What is it like in England? We hear that there is much crime and poverty." He tapped one side of his predatory nose. "We do not believe everything we hear."

Such spirit, in this case incited a little by the fire water, was always apparent in the outposts farthest away from the Kremlin. The wonder was that such people put up with Moscow's stuffy edicts at all. But such uncharacteristic obedience has always been one of the puzzles of history.

In the case of the Russians it is, perhaps, relatively easy to understand. Beneath their banners, red against the snow, they overthrew a tyranny, and so intoxicated were they by their victory that they realised too late that they had installed an even more merciless regime. And in World War II, having lost twenty million souls, they were too weakened to stand up to the regime which had steadily entrenched itself during the bloodshed.

But still these wild-tongued Siberians imparted hope. If such spirit flourished elsewhere within the fifteen republics then surely the Kremlin could not impose its iron will forever? Genuine patriotism might one day have its fling.

But, as always, I was reduced to one fundamental question: how can Communists elsewhere in the world still worship an ideology that has manifestly failed to improve the lives of ordinary people? Are they all as simple-minded as those who were subsequently to applaud the dispatch of doves of peace into the sky over the Olympic Stadium in Moscow while their hosts gunned down peasants in Afghanistan?

But no one was in the mood for politics tonight. I heard how the Siberians skied and sledded into infinity; how their children planted the city's silver-birch saplings in soil frozen as hard as concrete; how they resented the chain-clanking legends of the old Siberia.

I danced again, drank more vodka and beer and floated away to the hotel barely aware of the cold crisping my nostrils and nipping my ears and the frozen stars glittering in the Siberian night.

Next morning I ordered a taxi through Boris, the Intourist guide, as square and sturdy as a pill-box, telling him that I wanted to tour the outskirts of the city where the apartment blocks dribbled away into log cabins which, in their turn, faded into the leafless birch and larch of the taiga. There must have been an instruction from above to let the eccentric correspondent have his way because, miraculously, I was allowed to travel without guide or interpreter. Perhaps they hoped that I would be shot by the Chinese.

Leaving Dima to his own bizarre devices, I climbed into the battered black taxi and, as though rehearsing for an amateur spy movie, mouthed the immortal words: "Take me to the border."

The driver regarded me through slitted eyes set in a fleshy face. He looked not unlike Brezhnev, I thought. He let loose a torrent of Russian and began to pick his nose with his thumb.

"The border," I said. "Take me to it."

He continued to pick away moodily, but I had been prepared for just such an Intourist ruse. I produced a map and pointed to the border.

He was unmoved. "*Niet,*" he said. With his thumb still up his nostril his voice had a hollow ring to it.

"*Da.*"

"*Niet*"

He climbed from the cab and returned five minutes later with a worried looking Boris.

"I want to go to the border," I said.

"But you said —"

"I know what I said. I want to extend my tour."

"It is very dangerous," he said.

"Codswallop," I said.

"No codswallop," he said, importantly. "In the River Amur we have sturgeon."

"Take me there," I said, last night's vodka still in my veins.

"You will wait a minute please."

He made a telephone call and returned looking surprised. "You may go," he said. I wondered whom I had impressed; perhaps it was Fred.

The taxi driver shrugged, removed his thumb from his

56

nostril and off we set to confront the Chinese.

The drive was tranquil enough. The snow was gathering its forces for its drive south; frost sugared the cushions of the forest and the fretwork eaves of the cabins, pale pink and blue, were warm in the sunshine. High up in the blue sky an eagle crossed from China to Russia and back again.

The driver finally stopped at the gates of a sanatorium named Friendship. I wasn't sure whether we had reached the actual border, but I was quite sure we weren't going to get any further.

A couple of armoured cars and a lorry full of troops rumbled past. At least they — and the scruffy bar near the Friendship — imparted the flavour of a border post (I later discovered that I had been within a mile of the frontier). We adjourned to the bar favoured by hunters where the driver ordered vodka and fingers of black bread smeared with red caviar. Toasts were proposed, glasses raised: here I was on the same latitude as Paris, drinking fire-water with tiger trappers in Siberia with, so it was said, two million Chinese waiting down the road to occupy the territory they claimed as their own. It was a little bizarre, especially when I learned from a hunter with broken teeth and a sea-urchin stubble on his jaw that shepherds with their flocks still crossed the border magnificently unimpressed by the acrimony of the two Communist giants.

Hard news had been a bit thin on the ground up until now but that afternoon I was able to file a colour story that made the foreign page lead complete with a mug-shot of our man in Siberia.

Dima was unusually broody on the return flight. To spare him any humiliation I didn't tax him with questions. But obviously the big hairy gentleman had failed to keep his appointment.

*　　*　　*

Dima and I, reinforced this time by Diane, made one more trip that autumn: we took the night train to Leningrad. The train was long, green, serpent-faced and slow but it always arrived on time, nosing remorselessly through the snow-flying night.

I was going to report a court case in which a British seaman, 28-year-old John Weatherley from Newcastle-upon-Tyne, had been charged with malicious hooliganism. He had been involved in a punch-up in a hotel after trying to chat up two Russian girls, not realising that one of them had been married only a few hours earlier.

Again it was hardly a story to transport me close to the soul of Russia but it did provide a chance to explore the majestically-brooding buildings of the city, the broad avenues dividing them, and the Winter Palace housing the Hermitage with its three million paintings and exhibits.

Many of the buildings still bore the scars of war. But which war — Revolution or World War II siege by the Germans — I didn't know. I always saw the Revolution in black and white, Lenin's face rising from the smoke of battle; the siege I saw painted in grey, white and red, starvation, snow and courage spilling across a great canvas embracing 890 days during which 200,000 civilians were killed by German shells and 630,000 died from starvation. The Russian hatred of the Germans was branded in stone, in every chip from a bullet, in every furrow gouged by the splinter of a shell.

We toured the Hermitage at speed, Gilbert Lewthwaite of the *Mail* in tow making exaggerated gestures of artistic appreciation. For my part museums and art galleries always induce symptoms of acute claustrophobia: the pictures meld into one, the guide's voice takes on the pitch of a clergyman intoning psalms, and I have to flee to the great outdoors.

We strolled the granite quays beside the Neva, we wandered down Nevsky Prospect and in the evenings we adjourned to the Astoria Hotel, a comfortable old museum-piece with a lift that struggled upwards as though hauled by a team of White Russians lashed by the *plet*. From our hotel bedrooms we filed our stories, miraculously making immediate contact with London the moment we jangled the ancient telephones.

Gilbert was, as always, dependably good company. Tall, with slightly crumpled features, he laboured mightily with the Russian language but even I, to whom every foreign language is a jumbled cacophany, could detect sharp-cornered North Country vowels surfacing in his exchanges. I didn't mind him learning the language, but did he have to practise it ordering meals? It could take two hours to get dinner: in Gilbert's hands it could take four.

The bar was occupied by groups of belligerent Finns who crossed the border to remind the Russians what a run they'd given them for their money back in 1939-40. They wore black trousers and white shirts and when they were drunk they sang a lot. But whatever truculent message was intended it was largely wasted because few understood their strange language.

After three days the case against John Weatherley was concluded. The prosecution asked the woman judge to put him away in a labour camp for two years; the judge let him off with eighteen months.

I felt sorry for him because if he'd been involved in a similar fracas in any other country he would have got away with a fine. But in Leningrad he was lucky: if he'd been a German he would probably have got life.

On our last night in Leningrad Gilbert and I were hijacked by two whores.

We had been touring the city, pleasantly relaxed after filing the last instalment of the story, intending later that evening to visit a nightclub called the White Nights — so named because in high summer in Leningrad there is virtually no darkness.

But first we had to pick up Diane who also believed that her cultural impressions of the city would not be complete without a visit to a nightclub. We hailed a taxi in the Nevsky Prospect and told the driver to take us to the Astoria Hotel. Glancing over his shoulder the driver launched into a familiar routine. "Are you American?"

"No, English."

"My favourite people." We would have been his favourite people if we had been Eskimos. "You like girls?"

Yes, we said, we liked girls all right but we had our own, thank you very much.

"I get you girls."

"No thanks —"

The driver swung the cab across a line of traffic and pulled up at the kerb. There, conjured up from nowhere by the wizard at the wheel, were two girls.

They were both plump and rouged, bouffant hair — one a redhead, one a blonde — covered by scarves tied beneath their chins. One opened the door and they both climbed in. The driver who had obviously had a lot of experience of degenerate Englishmen said: "They are good girls. They are both goers as you say."

"Then tell them to go away," I told him.

He responded by letting out the clutch abruptly. Into our laps fell the two goers giggling and chatting away in Russian.

"What are they saying?" I asked Gilbert.

"God knows," said Gilbert from behind a filigree of starched blonde hair. "Your place or mine, I think."

I prodded the driver in the back. "Take us to the Astoria Hotel," I shouted in his ear.

"No good there," he said. "No pokey-pokey."

The girls were making themselves comfortable, skirts riding high, and whispering incomprehensible endearments in our ears.

"I have your number," I said to the driver. "If you don't

take us to the Astoria I shall report you to the police."

"The police?"

"Yes," I said, "the police."

He swung the wheel, completed a U-turn and, swearing venomously in Russian, headed in the direction of the hotel. The girls, sensing that the seduction was not going well, sat up and stared petulantly out of the window.

As we drew up outside the hotel Diane emerged and stared with mounting interest at the spectacle in the back of the cab. I opened a door and pushed the two girls out into the cold.

They stood for a moment jabbering excitedly. When Diane climbed into the taxi they made gestures that needed no translating and disappeared.

"Take us to the White Nights," I told the driver.

"But I thought —"

"To the White Nights," I said firmly and began my explanation to Diane. It took a long time.

V

The bitterest pill of all for the devout Communist to swallow in Moscow was the discovery that privilege flourished as healthily there as it did in a Capitalist state.

As the housewife waited patiently in queues reminiscent of war-time Britain, Kremlin wives, Party officials and intelligentsia (journalists even) plundered the *beryozka* shops stacked with imported luxuries.

While the assembly line worker waited years for delivery of a small car, the Kremlin élite belted down the middle of the streets in their Zil or Chaika limousines.

In the general hospitals the poor fought the germs that thrived in dirt, while in the Kremlin Clinic the rich recuperated in antiseptic comfort.

A family of six bargained and cajoled for a two-roomed apartment with a shared bathroom while movie actors or ballet stars relaxed in their dachas in Vnukovo or Zhukovka.

True, you could still travel for a few kopecks on the subway and rent a flat for about five pounds a month and take a holiday on the Black Sea for a pittance. But so could the privileged.

Among the semi-privileged were foreign diplomats, businessmen and journalists, particularly those from the West.

The Cubans seemed to fare the worst. But they accepted their inferior treatment philosophically, trudging gamely around in their baggy uniforms and retaliating by selling the

Russians abominable cigars that disintegrated inside their cellophane wrapping.

But even in our privileged ranks there were dissenters. They had to drink French champagne "not that chemical Russian rubbish", they had to import Earl Grey tea from Fortnum and Mason's and canned salmon from Alaska although it leaps into the tins from the rivers of Siberia.

Teeth also brought out the worst in us privileged foreigners. No one ever sought dental treatment in Moscow because you were liable to emerge from the surgery with a set of shining steel teeth. Instead we took ourselves to Helsinki. It cost a fortune but at least you didn't emerge with molars like plough-shares.

As Christmas approached Diane suddenly developed acute toothache. In the evening her face was its normal petal-shape; by next morning it looked like a pumpkin.

She telephoned Valerie Lewthwaite, a lovely ex-nurse with a temperament as tranquil as a dew-pond, and together they took off for the Finnish capital. I drove them to the railway station in Moscow and fondly kissed Diane on her good cheek.

Within five minutes I felt a faint throb in my upper jaw. By the following morning the swelling in my face had closed one eye.

My punishment, perhaps, for abusing privilege?

*   *   *

Like other Westerners we began to hoard the fruits of these privileges a long time before Christmas. A lot of the turkeys and plum puddings were either air-freighted from London or dispatched by rail from Helsinki. If your newpaper or country was out of favour with the Kremlin then it could be a long wait before Customs allowed you to collect your prizes. If, for instance, the British Foreign Office had delivered a rude note to the Soviet Ambassador in London, then your documents were predictably out of order.

At Kutuzovsky Prospect we managed to stock a decent larder and waited curiously to see how the anniversary of the birth of Christ would be celebrated in an atheist land. In fact the Russians proved to be schizophrenic about it. They accepted its mood, denied its origins, introduced a substitute Santa Claus — Grandfather Frost — and finally celebrated the New Year.

Fresh snow fell at night, lighting the bedroom with a bluish glow that rekindled the winter dawns of childhood. And every day of the holiday the sun shone from a polished sky finding jewels in the ground's ermine mantle. At dusk the cold crept back from its lair trapping powdered snow in the halos of the street lamps.

Water had been hosed onto part of the prison camp car-park and in the evenings we watched the Scandinavians and Canadians and their children skating by floodlight beside the ranks of snow-bonneted cars. Sometimes they lit a fire and, as the sparks spiralled into the night, we would catch sight of a fur-hatted sentry peering enviously into our festive privacy and we felt like pioneers surrounded by covered wagons.

Dima, Vladimir and Valentina approached our Christmas with an initial correctitude that dispersed after they had sampled our hot toddy. We played them scratched carols on the record player, stuck a branch of a pine tree in a bucket filled with sand and festooned it with decorations left over from the Revolution. On the Chi Chi bar we paraded our Christmas cards, having taken the precaution to send each other a few to swell the numbers.

On the day before Christmas Eve, traditionally the time for Fleet Street festivities since few journalists or printers work on 24th December — there aren't any papers on Christmas Day — we threw a party.

We invited Fred, and although he didn't put in an appearance, a few Russians from Novosti and the UPKD did. By midnight staid Western diplomats were dancing Cossack style, hitherto remote wives were pouring jugs of water over each other and one couple were draped over the Tass machine in a feverish embrace.

Under the table I found a Canadian diplomat, in whose apartment I had once noticed a book called *Manners and Etiquette*, taking shelter while his elegantly gowned wife poured a tankard of mulled wine inside the trousers of a whooping Soviet bureaucrat.

As the party broke up we heard cries of dismay from the couple utilising the Tass machine in the spare kitchen. Just as their passions were reaching a crisis the insensitive apparatus had apparently started to punch out a story about encouraging trade figures in Uzbekistan.

Christmas Eve was another glittering day and we drove to Peredelkino, the writers' colony to the south-west of the city, to visit the grave of Pasternak. The stark, snowcapped tomb bore an engraving of the author's tormented features and the legend *Boris Pasternak, 1890-1960*.

The plot, sheltered by pine and birch trees, was untended although a few jars containing frostbitten flowers, their blossoms like crumpled lace handkerchiefs, stood at the base of the gravestone. In one corner of the plot stood a smaller tomb in memory of his wife. Both of them forlorn and apparently forgotten, which was just how the Kremlin leaders, who had forced Pasternak to refuse the Nobel Prize because his novel *Dr Zhivago* didn't totally reflect the glory of the Revolution, wanted it. Except, of course, that they would have liked to bury Dr Zhivago as well.

That evening Dima presented me with a small statue of a Russian bear and Diane with a pair of woollen slippers. Vladimir gave us a beautiful lacquer box; Valentina produced two dozen mince pies slugged, I suspected, with vodka.

We shook hands and embraced in the flickering lights of our spindly Christmas *tree*. Diane and I sang a couple of carols while Vladimir reached deep down into his barrel chest to release rich, sad songs from the taiga.

On Christmas Day we drove to an apartment in another foreign ghetto where John Miller of the *Telegraph* and his pretty blonde wife Brenda lived. The Lewthwaites were there with their children, the Miller children were there and so, therefore, was the soul of Christmas.

John, with his straight dark hair and spectacles, was deceptively studious. But with his command of Russian he was able more than most to redicule pretentious Soviet spokesmen. He was also able to dictate a column of immaculate copy at a formidable speed. He was a competitor to respect but today, as he carved the turkey wearing a funny hat, he was Mr Pickwick without the paunch.

The day was soon snuffed out by dusk and back we went to our big battered apartment. We switched off the Tass machine, as intrusive as a spoilt child, played *Swan Lake* on the record player and lit our Swedish candles.

From the bar a model of Grandfather Frost regarded us benignly. Or was it Santa Claus? It didn't really seem to matter.

* * *

Privileges such as we and Soviet VIP's enjoyed weren't the only aspects of Russian life that would have dismayed the shiny-eyed idealist seeking the benefits to humanity envisaged by Karl Marx and Vladimir Ilyich Lenin. He would, for instance, have discovered more drunks in Moscow than in Dublin on a Saturday night and a crime rate that kept the prisons packed.

The vodka consumption was prodigious and the drunks reeled and collapsed dramatically in the streets even though they tried to absorb the fierce liquor with bread, pickled cucumber, salami, herring and beetroot.

Some students of Russian behaviour claim that they drink to forget the tedium of their everyday lives and the shortage of creature comforts. I got the impression that they drank to get drunk.

There was a calculated intensity about their drinking parties that is absent from a Western booze-up. Snacks were laid out, glasses lined up, bottles placed on the assembly line, any articles with which they might later crack each other's skulls removed from sight.

I attended one such party which proceeded along classic lines. A swashbuckling toast and straight down the throat went the first measure of vodka to lie smouldering in my stomach until I dispatched a snack to join it. After two or three such toasts my host, a poet, with a pugilist's chin and fists like hams, lectured me earnestly about the advantages of the Soviet System.

"It is the future that matters," he said giving me an unpoetic prod in the chest with one thick finger. "It is always the future, is it not? But you in the West have to worry, worry, worry about it. You worry about unemployment, you worry about old age. Here we do not worry about it. We are always paid whether we are out of work, sick or old."

I suspected that he was paid rather more than most because the apartment was a salon expensively furnished with deep-polished mahogany furniture and cut-glass mirrors but, such was the shine on his knuckles, I kept my counsel.

"You see," he went on, downing another vodka and munching a slice of pickled cucumber, "we have much to look forward to. We realise that our standards of living don't compare with yours so we look forward to improvement. We have lived for so long with poverty that we are delighted with any small comfort."

He belched loudly and with satisfaction. "And why have we been deprived for so long?" he asked.

Knowing by now what was coming I said timidly: "The last war?"

"Exactly. But not *just* the last war," he was mildly irritated that I had found the answer so quickly. "We had a revolution, remember. We endured great hardship, we Russian bears. Then came the war. Do you know how many souls we lost? Twenty million," he shouted before I could answer.

And, of course, he had a point; oft-stated but nonetheless valid. Russia had suffered as only Mother Russia can. But I never heard anyone ever discuss how West Germany had come to rise so triumphantly from the ashes of the same war.

After a couple more vodkas the mood of my host and the other guests, young men and women, reputedly intelligentsia, changed. Boisterousness and belligerence overtook them as doctrinaire drowned in vodka — a home made brew, apparently, manufactured by a student chemist.

A girl with braided black hair and dark eyes turned on the host and said in heavily accented English: "The war, always it is the war. If you fell under a bus you would blame the war."

The poet considered this, jutting out his chin agressively, then said surprisingly: "You are right, to hell with the war," and clumped a heavy arm over my shoulders. "We drink," he cried, splashing vodka into everyone's glasses, "we drink to peace. To hell with wars."

After this pacific toast someone threw a glass against the wall. It made a satisfying sound, a reverberation of Tsarist excesses. Where were the balalaikas, the dancing gypsies and Greta Garbo? I was surprised how sober I was remaining.

By now a lachrymose note was entering the festivities. At first the songs had been robust, now the voices were diluted with tears. Tragedy was stalking in our midst. As the girl with the braided hair evoked some dismal picture from the Ukraine in a deep contralto voice, the poet's great chin sank lower on his chest. "Life," he informed me, "is a burden from birth to death."

"It wasn't just now," I reminded him but he ignored me.

A young man on my right who looked like a poet but was in fact a military historian whispered to me conspiratorially: "First he lectures, then he laughs. Next he cries, finally he fights."

"What makes him fight?" I asked.

"Foreigners," said the military historian.

"Perhaps," I said carefully, "I should go." I wanted to say: "It's just about my bed-time," but as it was only eight in the evening this was an unlikely pretext for departure.

"You *want* to leave?"

"I thought perhaps I should."

"That will make him want to fight even more. He hates people who leave his parties early."

Miserably I twiddled my empty glass. The poet noticed the movement and refilled it. I tossed it back with a flourish and heard myself shouting: "Bottoms up folks." And then, aware that this might be misinterpreted: "Skin off all your noses."

"Is that all you have to say?" the poet asked, an ominous frown creasing his forehead. "Skin off the noses?"

"It's a common toast in the West," I told him.

"But why skin off the noses? Are you sure it isn't just for us Russian peasants, this skin off the noses?"

No, I assured him, the cream of English artistocracy often proposed such a toast.

"Ah, the aristocracy." An ugly note entered his voice. "In Russia we say *kaput* to all the aristocracy."

"They're pretty thin on the ground in England," I said.

"It doesn't matter," he said, "they are all big shits."

I nodded vigorously.

"You agree with me?"

"But of course."

"But you must not," he said piteously. "We cannot agree. How can we fight if we agree all the time?"

"You will just have to find someone else to fight," I said, sounding like a sensible English nanny.

He tossed back another vodka and considered this unwelcome advice. "You think all aristocrats are big shits?"

"Enormous ones," I said.

He groaned deeply as gravity once more dragged his chin towards his chest. "It is too much," he said.

Opposite me the girl with the braids was weeping helplessly while a bearded man beside her thoughtfully massaged her breasts. The military historian whispered to me the unwelcome news, "Soon the eruption will come."

Suddenly the poet rose to his feet, leaned across my bowed head, shouted to the military historian: "You have insulted my English friend," and punched him on the ear.

At this stage I decided that it would be unwise to place any further strain on Anglo–Soviet relations and, on the pretext of visiting the bathroom, slipped out of the apartment while the military historian was rubbing his ear and planning his strategy.

I didn't get far. I had been warned about the delayed effects of vodka but had barely heeded them. When I entered the elevator on the twelfth floor I was in a euphoric mood; when I reached the ground floor I was unconscious.

It was later calculated that I must have been up and down the apartment block in the elevator accompanied by residents who thought it diplomatic not to disturb me half a dozen times before I was rescued.

I fared better at least than two other guests at the party who were apprehended by the police and carted off to one of the sobering-up stations — grim but practical institutes where the more bibulous Muscovites are hosed down before being dried out.

Several weeks later I visited one of these establishments housed in a derelict monastery. It was a haunted place overlooking the river; its domes were as fragile as parchment, its bricks gnawed by the teeth of many winters. The chapel had been used as a storehouse and it smelled of distemper and stagnation and, faintly, of incense as though someone had been secretly worshipping there.

The monastery was being restored for the convenience of its new inebriate congregation. Railings had been planted around the buildings and, above the entrance to the chapel, the face of Christ had been resurrected in chipped mosaic. On the snow lay faded icons and rusty crosses.

The sobering-up premises adjoined the chapel, an incongruous juxtaposition but Moscow abounded with such anolomies. The American Club had once been a morgue and there were those who suggested that it still was. The disadvantage of this positioning was that the first sight beheld by those drunks who were still conscious was the features of Christ gazing reproachfully at them. Believing that they were in heaven — a paradise which they had been led to believe did not exist — they fell in belated postures of worship which infuriated the staff.

I drove to the monastery on a Sunday, the only day I could escape the vigilance of Dima who would not have condoned the excursion. It was a bleak day, the snow hard on the ground. I was met at the door by a scowling, pouchy-eyed man who looked as though he had contracted the combined hangovers of his customers.

I waved a bundle of passes and documents in front of his face and muttered a few guttural phrases that I had rehearsed that morning. Miraculously he let me in. But Sunday was apparently a bad day for business, a day of rest from the bottle, because the place was empty.

The clinic consisted of two rooms. One contained a shower, some lockers and half a dozen beds; the other medicines, salves and bandages with which to treat those who had hurt themselves and straps with which to bind the more animated reprobates to their beds.

But the principal restorative was the shower. The drunks were held forcibly under its nozzle and subjected to a blast of ice-cold water; only the most indomitable boozers emerged from this pitiless deluge still throwing punches. Shivering despite the heat, I bade farewell to the morose custodian and returned thankfully to the clean breath of the outdoors.

I have heard it argued that there is much to be said for these institutions; that their incisive treatment is preferable to the long wait in police cells followed by the ignominy of a court appearance.

Perhaps. But as I climbed back into the Cortina, I vowed that, should I ever subside in the gutter singing ribald songs, I would make damn sure I was in London rather than Moscow.

*   *   *

Crime was mostly of the kind that always partners scarcity. Bribery, black-marketeering, graft. The Russians had one word for it all — *blat*. And it was as rampant as it had been in England during World War II.

The *blat* most commonly encountered by the foreigner was the offer by a street spiv to buy his clothes or his hard currency at outrageously inflated rates.

I was once approached in Gorky Park by a sallow young man with a downy moustache who pointed at my trousers — rather a flash pair fashioned in Prince of Wales check — and suggested I accompany him into a copse. Suspecting that he was a homosexual soliciting — the practice was not uncommon in the precincts of the Bolshoi — I strode imperiously on my way with Dima at my side.

When we had escaped I asked Dima what he wanted. "He wanted to buy your trousers," Dima said.

"And what was I supposed to have worn if I had sold him my trousers?"

"His," Dima said simply.

But you had to be extremely naïve to encourage such deals. In Leningrad, a young American ex-serviceman was convicted of selling thirty-five dollars and thirty-five Finnish marks for roubles. He had also removed an ornament from his hotel, but it was a trophy rather than plunder.

For the two offences he was sentenced to three years in a labour camp.

VI

Second only to avoiding predatory Russians, the most difficult manoeuvre for a foreigner in Moscow is approaching law-abiding citizens. I discovered this when the foreign desk asked me to interview the Man in the Street and get his views on *détente* between the West and the Soviet bloc.

When I told Dima what we had to do he began to polish his spectacles vigorously, a sure sign that he was worried. Finally he told me that he did not consider this to be a particularly good idea.

"It's not for us to reason why," I informed him.

"They won't like it, you know."

"Why on earth not? It's *détente* we're talking about, not a threat to drop an H-bomb on Moscow."

Dima smiled grimly, planting his fur hat firmly on his head like a soldier putting on a tin helmet before going over the top and led the way outside.

It was snowing and the pedestrians on Kutuzovsky Prospect were leaning into the wind like sailors in a storm. I pointed out a man wearing an expensive sealskin hat, black coat and goloshes. "Go and ask him what he thinks about *détente*," I commanded Dima.

Dima went after his prey. The man spun round as though a gun had been jabbed in his back and Dima addressed him, nodding in my direction as though I were an amiable lunatic.

74

Finally the man threw up his hands and stalked off into the falling snow.

"Well," I asked Dima, "what did he say?"

"I don't know," Dima said.

"What do you mean you don't know?"

"He was Polish," Dima said.

Did I detect a gleam of satisfaction in his eye?

"Well try again," I told him. "A woman this time."

"A woman?"

"Yes, Dima, a woman."

"She will think I am accosting her."

"She will be very flattered. Here comes a likely looking customer," I added, as a sturdy looking woman wearing felt boots, two overcoats and a scarf as thick as a carpet wrapped round her head materialised out of the snow.

"I don't —"

"Get in there, Dima."

He approached her as furtively as a vendor of dirty post-cards and, once again nodding in my direction, put the question. She responded by balling one mittened fist under his nose and, with her other hand, giving him a violent push.

Reporting back, Dima said: "Well, you saw what happened?"

"Didn't she say anything?"

"Oh yes," Dima said, "she said something all right. But you couldn't put it in the newspaper."

"Well, we'll just have to try again."

"You mean," said Dima, a note of rebellion in his voice, "that I will just have to try again."

He made three more swoops in rapid succession and was rebuffed on each occasion.

"It's hopeless," he told me.

"I think you're right. Try just once more."

He approached a young man with a bandit's face and was

75

rewarded by a torrent of abuse.

"What did he say?" I asked as, beaten and dejected, we returned to the apartment in the lift.

"He thought you were American," Dima said. "It's bad enough saying you're British but when they think you're an American in disguise it's hopeless."

Which I knew to be true. Vietnam tainted all Russians' opinions of the United States and Gary Powers' U-2 spy plane was still on display to the public.

Back in the apartment I had an inspiration. "Dima," I said, "what do you think about *détente*?"

He looked at me suspiciously. "Am I supposed to be your Man in the Street?"

"Why not?"

"No thanks," he said.

"But you must have some opinion about it."

"No comment to make to the Press," he said and made for the door.

However, the barriers between the Russian people and foreigners were not quite as insurmountable as some observers made them out to be. Many Muscovites spoke English and it only needed the right catalyst to draw them out.

One such catalyst was sport. As a lifetime spectator rather than a participant I attended as many football matches as I could. Along with me went Diane. A French-Canadian who appreciated soccer? Surely a unique phenomenon!

The games were even-tempered, the crowds well-behaved, confining their displeasure to whistling. As soon as a neighbour in the crowd realised that I was English he felt compelled to ask me if I supported Arsenal. As it happened I did; the discovery dispelled all inhibitions and for the rest of the match, in between cheers and whistles, we chatted away about the relative merits of the Gunners and the Dynamos.

No Muscovite that I ever met expressed much interest in

Manchester United or Liverpool. Why Arsenal merited such a following I never discovered: perhaps it was their colours.

I also attended chess tournaments where all the spectators, irrespective of nationality, were joined in agonising suspense. To the Russians chess was more than just a game; it was a dedication. It was taught at school, it helped to digest the long winter and it was known affectionately as "the great time-waster."

In the tournament halls mass concentration and intensity of feeling quivered on the hot air. Several games were played simultaneously, each move recorded on enlarged magnetic boards on the walls. On the stage the players brooded over their black and white armies, attacked or withdrew strategically, rang up the time on their clocks and either relaxed with apparent indifference to their opponent's machinations or paced up and down as restlessly as big cats in a cage.

As each move was recorded by small boys on the boards on the walls, the spectators, seated or standing close-packed at the rear of the hall, sighed or hugged themselves in exquisite torment. One coversational ploy was to suggest a move you thought one of the masters should make. If this was transparently absurd you were ignored, but if there was at least some wisdom in it you were rewarded by a counter comment, and you had made contact.

Once a grand master playing white took fifteen minutes to make his opening move. An astonishing display of procrastination by any standards. Finally, with the air of a man who had made an innovative contribution to the game, the grand master played the most common opening move of all, pawn to king four. The spectators applauded wildly.

Next day I consulted the chess expert at UPI, a Russian who had been covering the tournament for the agency. "Why," I asked, "did he take so long to make his first move?"

The Russian hesitated for a moment, reluctant to tarnish the image of the game. Then he shrugged eloquently and said: "Because he had a hangover."

Ice-hockey was also a sport that could ignite instant communication, although not necessarily in the convivial sense. The trouble, as in other sports, was that although the competitors were all supposed to be amateurs the Russians most decidedly weren't: they were paid with dollar coupons which enabled them to buy luxury goods and given automobiles, superior accommodation and other privileges.

International encounters, therefore, were often a farce. In the case of Canada, for instance, the best ice-hockey players had, naturally enough, become professionals leaving the second-best, the amateurs, to play Russia which was, in fact, fielding its first team. The result: the true amateurs were slaughtered.

Feelings came to a head one evening in the dollar bar of the National Hotel where, unwisely, the Canadians and the Russians had agreed to meet to toast sportsmanship. This bar was a bizarre place, with gold-papered walls, cafeteria tables and blonde barmaids with beehive hairstyles who served every drink diluted with Narzan mineral water. Its purpose was to relieve Westerners of hard currency and, after sufficient quantities of Scotch and Narzan had been consumed, a few plump whores were allowed in to finish off the job.

I went along with Diane because there were Canadians present and she had followed ice-hockey and could debate the skills of Bobby Orr with them. At the bar sat the usual medley of nationalities, Third World emissaries, Western business men drowning their frustrations, journalists, a British MP waiting for an interview with Kosygin which he had never been promised, a couple of KGB officers tuning their invisible antennae. At the tables Russians and Canadians were mixing boisterously, hugging each other, administering playful punches and smiting imaginary pucks with imaginary sticks.

Just as Diane and I were about to leave, a crew cut Canadian with muscles pushing his blazer out of shape said to a Russian: "One thing's for sure, you guys have got it made."

"Yes," said the Russian who was a big as the Canadian, "we have got it made. But so have you."

"Sure we have. But we earn our dough."

"So do we," said the Russian, puzzled.

"You do, huh? What's your line of business, Ivan?"

"I am an interpreter," said the Russian coldly.

"But you told me you had a great apartment, an automobile, a place in the country. Not bad for an interpreter . . . I figured they made lousy money."

"You figured wrong," said the Russian. Other members of his team were assembling behind him; one of the barmaids was calling the police. The British MP departed.

The Canadian shook his head belligerently. "I figured right. You make your goddam money playing hockey. Isn't that right, Ivan? You're pros, the whole bunch of you, and that's how you win. But I tell you this, put you up against the Canadian pros and you wouldn't even reach first base."

Even I knew that he was confusing his games.

The Russian said: "You're drunk," and gave him a push.

"Don't do that again," said the Canadian. "Just don't ever do that again."

The Russian did it again and a classic bar-room brawl broke out. A mirror broke, glasses and bottles smashed, the whores, bouffant hair demolished, joined in; men hit the walls and slid to the floor, beatific smiles on their faces; friends hit friends instead of enemies who had ducked. Only the pianist playing unperturbably through it all was missing. Diane and I watched from the wings until the police arrived. The combatants were parted but no proceedings were taken. After all, the toast had been sportsmanship.

Another catalyst that encouraged conversation was the

Russians' hatred of the Germans. Whereas their hostility towards the Americans and British had an indoctrinated ring about it, their bitterness towards the Germans burned like acid.

They had been betrayed by the Germans and that betrayal had cost them twenty million souls. And it was the women who hated the deepest. There they were scraping the snow from the pavements, painting apartment blocks, feeding assembly lines, and always returning to homes bereft of husbands and sons killed by the Germans.

To get my hair cut I used to cross Kutuzovsky to the great hulk of the Ukraina Hotel where half a dozen women in white spent their days scalping foreigners. If you were German you were lucky to escape with your ears.

Already primed about their ferocity, I went there accompanied by Dima and immediately launched into a diatribe about the Germans, the common enemy that the Soviet Union — assisted by America and Britain — had defeated in the war. The hairdresser, built in Valentina's mould, paused, shearing scissors in her hand. "You are German?" she asked ominously.

"Good God, tell her no," I shouted as Dima finished translating. "Tell her I detest them."

"All right, all right," Dima said soothingly.

The scissors stopped switching.

"Tell her," I went on, "that the Germans dropped a bomb on my house during the war." (This wasn't strictly true: a fifty-pound bomb had landed in our neighbour's garden and shifted their garage a distance of twenty yards). "And tell her I don't want my hair cut too short."

When this information was imparted the woman cradled my head against her bosom and began to snip away as gently as though I were her first-born child.

*   *   *

Many contacts with Russians produced examples of kindness and courtesy completely at odds with their granite image.

One chilled afternoon I went to Dyetsky Mir, the huge children's store incongruously situated opposite Lubyanka Prison, to buy a birthday present for a friend's small son. This was a far more formidable excursion than a visit to Selfridges. First you stood in a queue at the counter where a girl calculated the bill on an abacus and gave you a ticket bearing the price; armed with this you joined another queue at the cash-desk; when you had paid her another girl stamped your ticket and you joined yet another queue to collect your purchase. Shopping at Dyetsky Mir could age you beyond your years.

I chose a model rocket, as primitive as the real Soviet hardware was sophisticated, and with my ticket joined the queue at the cash-desk. It wasn't until I faced the clerk, a businesslike blonde, that I discovered that I had left all my money in the apartment. Not only that but I hadn't brought Dima with me to explain. The blonde grabbed my ticket and waited expectantly for the cash. "*Niet,*" I said. "*Niet* money," pulling out the insides of my coat pockets in a feeble mime of poverty.

She glared at me, then asked in passable English: "Are you British?" as though that would explain everything.

I nodded eagerly and told her that I had left my wallet on the dressing table.

"The toy . . . Is it for your son?"

"For a friend's little boy."

"It is his birthday, yes?"

"He's six today," I told her.

"I have a son aged six," she said and from her handbag produced the price of the rocket in crumpled rouble notes. "You pay me tomorrow," she said.

As I departed her stern features had softened as she thought of her son.

On another occasion I went to the indoor market on Tsvetnoy Boulevard to buy Diane a bunch of roses. The building was as cavernous as a corn exchange, stalls piled high with fruit, vegetables and flowers from Georgia. Everything was exorbitantly expensive but I had been advised that you were expected to haggle.

At a stall kept by an emaciated man smoking a cigarette which was cupped in his hand convict fashion I pointed at some red roses, their buds just unfurling, and told Dima to ask him how much they were.

They were one rouble (about 40 pence) each, he told us. With bravado born of the fact that Dima was doing the dirty work I offered fifty kopecks.

A voluble exchange followed. The stallholder gesticulated wildly, his thin features suddenly animated, and savagely ground his cigarette on the ground with the heel of his boot. Finally he selected a dozen roses and wrapped them in tin foil.

"What's happening?" I asked Dima plaintively.

"He asked if you were English," Dima told me.

"And?"

"He said he likes the English. He met some Tommies in Berlin during the war."

"So how much has he knocked off the price?" I asked, hard-hearted businessman that I was.

"He says they are a gift," Dima said. "For old times' sake. And you must accept them as a gift," Dima said with uncharacteristic asperity, "or you will hurt his feelings."

But one of the most warming displays of kindness occurred at the Bolshoi.

When I handed in my sheepskin coat at the cloakroom the girl attendant searched in vain for the tag with which to hang it on a hook. Diane, already able to mouth a pocket-dictionary full of Russian, explained that it had been torn off. When I collected the coat after the ballet I found that a new tag had been sewn onto the lining with tiny, painstaking stitches.

"It was nothing," said the attendant. She just couldn't bear the thought of such a fine garment lying on the floor. I tried to pay her but she refused to accept any money. "Just tell him to remember me every time he hangs up his coat," she told Diane. And so I did and still do even though these days it is a different coat.

Not all Muscovites, of course, were such models of civility and compassion.

Round the corner from the apartment stood a café that, in an article by a colleague on another newspaper, had earned itself the title The Rudest Restaurant in the World. Business immediately boomed, customers vying with each other to receive the most contemptuous treatment, the most scandalous insult. One evening Diane and I decided to find out what degree of boorishness we merited.

The building was suitably ugly, a square box of steel, glass and cement; inside it was as steamy and noisy as a works canteen. When we put our coats on the counter the cloakroom attendant continued to read his newspaper and pick his teeth with a split match. We cleared our throats noisily until he finally looked up and reluctantly focussed his eyes on us. Satisfied that we were indeed customers he slid off his stool and disappeared through a door at the back of the room. Five minutes later he returned, grabbed our coats, tossed us a ticket and returned to the newspaper and the split match.

Inside the restaurant the head waiter, wearing a food-stained blue jacket and crumpled black trousers, slouched up to us and told us the place was full.

"But it isn't," I said to Diane pointing at some empty tables. "See what he's got to say about them."

Diane spoke to him and told me: "He says he can't see any empty tables. But I think I can handle him," she added, rounding tigerishly on the fugitive from the Marx Brothers.

I heard words like Politburo and Intourist and finally he grudgingly led us to one of the tables. Half an hour later a table-cloth was thrown over the plastic surface followed by knives, forks and spoons. When Diane complained that her knife was dirty the waiter, a new-comer with larded hair and a perspiring face, wiped it on the seat of his trousers.

Fifteen minutes later he tossed a menu on the table with the air of a punter discarding a worthless betting slip and stood, pad and pencil in hand, staring through the streaming window. Playing safe, we ordered chicken-noodle soup and steak and chips.

For the first time his expression indicated that he occasionally found pleasure in his calling. There was no chicken-noodle soup, he said, nor was there any steak.

Pea soup? *Niet*. Lamb chops? *Niet*. A faint smile crossed his features.

"Ask him what there is," I told Diane.

She asked him and he shrugged, a beautiful stage shrug that implored an unseen audience to sympathise with him in his predicament. Why should a waiter, of all people, know what was available on a menu?

"You'd better do your Politburo bit again," I said.

"I'll do better," Diane said. She unleashed a torrent of Russian and the waiter stepped back, new respect on his features, like a street fighter who has met his match. He mumbled a few faltering phrases and disappeared through the swing doors leading to the kitchens.

Diane said: "We're having chicken and chips and cabbage soup."

"What did you say to him?"

"I told him he was a sonofabitch."

"Is that all?"

"A few other things besides," she said.

When the waiter returned half an hour later the fight was

back in him. He managed to slop soup over my trousers and knocked the salt-cellar on Diane's lap with an adroit movement of his elbow.

When he arrived with the main course he tipped a few chips onto my crotch and was turning, about to make a run for the kitchens, when I caught his arm.

"Tell him," I said to Diane, "that this isn't chicken. It looks more like moose."

This time even I understood the exchange.

"This isn't chicken."

"It's chicken."

"I say it isn't."

"Say what you like, it's chicken."

"Bring us some chicken."

"You've already got chicken."

Diane forked a slice of meat and held it under his nose. "Is that chicken?"

"That's chicken all right."

I let go of his arm. "It's useless," I said. "We might as well eat the chips and clear off."

The waiter rotated his arm as though I had dislocated it and walked away with the swagger of a triumphant bullfighter. We finished our chips and departed.

Next day, before the British Embassy Press briefing, I compared notes with other journalists about the varying degrees of insolence we had experienced. One reporter who swore that the cloakroom attendant had brushed his coat with a lavatory brush appeared to be an outright winner until I asked what reprisals he had taken.

"Reprisals?" He stared at me malevolently. "What reprisals could there possibly be?"

"We didn't pay," I said.

A few weeks later revenge of a sort was exacted on the Press.

But none of us really understood its motivation because, if Press criticism of the restaurant was the culprit, then it was surely an absurd case of overkill.

The victim was a girl from an American paper who visited the establishment with two friends. They ordered a carafe of vodka, filled their glasses and were then lured away from the table on some pretext or other. When the girl returned she was perfectly sober. One swallow from her glass of vodka and she was transformed into a classic music-hall drunk.

Two waiters helped her to her feet and led her to the door where she stood swaying and leaning on them while cameramen who had appeared miraculously took pictures. The photograph was prominently displayed in the Soviet Press as an example of Western decadence.

Obviously her drink had been spiked in her absence. But why such an elaborate charade should have been staged no one could understand. Happily her employers didn't believe one word of the Soviet version of the incident. But subsequently the Press went elsewhere to be insulted.

VII

Winter in Moscow was divided into two mini-seasons. The first was the poet's winter when the snow still fell in Christmas flakes and fingers of it fell softly from branches of the trees; the second belonged to the pioneer — the snow fell sparsely, as hard as shot, and soiled dunes of it were piled high on the pavements.

It was during the first period that we lost Peter Worthington.

While he pored over the chess-board, honed Indian features intent, his mind, it materialised, had been debating greater issues than any gambit devised by Lars or myself; he had been considering the Great Escape.

Peter's interpreter was a woman, efficient and attractive. I don't know the reasons for what transpired. Perhaps she baulked at the lot of a woman in Soviet Society at that time. They carried out men's work, practised birth control by legal abortion and, so it was said, were not expected to enjoy sex. (When I mentioned foreplay to a Russian male he thought it was a game of cards.)

Perhaps she saw life, Western style, in Peter's newspapers and magazines and coveted it — an omnipresent temptation to all the interpreters. Whatever the reason, she made it known to Peter during their professional relationship that she wished to defect.

She then left Russia on vacation and the first I knew of any looming crisis was when Vladimir, my sparring partner from the KGB-controlled Novosti, inquired whether I had received any news of her.

Why should I have? I regarded him over the rim of my glass of vodka with surprise. And it was only much later, when it was established that she had defected, that I realised that Vladimir wondered if Peter had confided in me.

Peter denied all knowledge of her disappearance and Lars and I believed him. But his mind must have been in considerable turmoil as he pushed his pawns down the board or braved the snow in minimal clothing.

To this day I'm not sure about his involvement in the defection. But even my naïvety was stretched when he overstayed an overseas vacation leaving behind his new Mercedes in Moscow. Then the girl turned up in Canada and Lars and I were left puzzling over our ingenuousness.

After the first shock had evaporated we realised that we hadn't in any way been betrayed. The opposite in fact: Peter hadn't wanted to involve us or burden us with the weight of clandestine knowledge. He was the most honourable of men and a genuine individual rather than a histrionic character. He subsequently came to be regarded not only as one of North America's leading authorities on Russia but also helped to found a newspaper.

In Moscow he had been representing a Toronto daily. When that newspaper folded up the redundant staff started up a rival publication to the *Toronto Star*. And because they believed that unions had been partly responsible for the collapse of their original newspaper they set up a computerised operation in which unions were not permitted to interfere.

When I last saw Peter in Toronto he was editor of this chipper tabloid which they called the *Sun*. But he had changed; he was wearing an overcoat.

During the bitter second half of winter there were many new arrivals to the city and to the apartment – and one spectacular departure.

Many of the visitors to the apartment were Russians dispatched to trap me into some devastating indiscretion. Such surveillance was routine, instigated by some KGB department that hadn't co-ordinated with Fred who knew by now that such ruses were doomed to failure.

One of them claimed to be a playwright. He had wild, woolly hair and brandished a manuscript which shed pages like autumn leaves. From time to time, as he underlined a telling phrase with his thumb-nail, he bellowed phrases such as "Down with the neo-Capitalists at the Kremlin," which Dima, looking acutely embarrassed, had to translate.

Finally he departed with the announcement: "And now I am going to terminate myself," which, I felt, lost something in Dima's low-key interpretation. From the kitchen window I watched him stride purposefully across the soiled snow and wave cheerily at the uniformed sentries.

That was the only brand of temptation to which I was subjected. Other correspondents were compromised in far more satisfying circumstances. One demure young lady visiting a correspondent on a cultural mission suddenly ripped open her blouse revealing a magnificent bosom, pulled up her skirt and, with thighs spread, collapsed on the sofa shouting that she had been raped.

Remembering a rape case long ago on a British Railways train, the correspondent showed the in-rushing KGB agents his cigarette on which a long stem of ash still remained. His passions, he pointed out, must have been pretty tepid if the ash hadn't toppled off in the fracas. The girl, he told me, quickly closed her thighs in case he absent-mindedly decided to dispose of the evidence and fled. Heady stuff compared with a visit by a demented playwright.

We were also visited by a succession of small-time defectors from the West, among them Len Wincott who had taken part in the last mutiny in the British Navy at Invergordon. He had subsequently fled from Capitalist persecution to the untrammelled freedoms of the Soviet Union where he had been persuaded to relinquish his passport. He served in the Red Army during World War II and as a reward was sentenced to a long term of imprisonment in a labour camp.

He was a sturdy, balding figure who looked like an ageing Welsh miner. Since his release from the camp he had settled comfortably into Muscovite life. He had been given a neat little apartment — an act of contrition, perhaps, by the State — and was happily married to a Russian woman of considerable grace and charm.

But from time to time he was assailed by home-sickness. He visited most of the British correspondents to read their air-mailed newspapers and he once asked a newspaperman taking a couple of weeks' leave to bring him back a matchbox filled with English soil.

All he wanted to do, he claimed, was briefly to visit the country of his birth. The Russians were willing to grant him an exit visa but the British wouldn't have him.

From time to time most of us wrote stories about Len and the intractable British Government who couldn't forgive a youthful act of rebellion committed decades earlier. There was no sign during my sojourn in Moscow that they would ever relent; but years later I read that he had been allowed to visit his homeland.

It was left to a visitor from Hayes, Middlesex, a bespectacled thirty-four year-old scientist named John Williams, to touch chords of romance discarded but not quite forgotten by Soviet bureaucrats.

He was taken around the tourist attractions of the Kremlin by a gorgeous, red-haired Intourist guide named Larissa

Zhuravlova — and fell in love with her. He proposed marriage and was accepted. But it seemed highly unlikely that the Russians would permit such a union. His pessimism was confounded and one icy morning Diane, Dima and I went to the Palace of Weddings to witness the nuptials.

They took eight minutes. It was a bleak little ceremony but in its way a triumph of compassion. The registrar was a woman. She was dressed in black and her chamber was empty except for a desk on which stood a bust of Lenin and a vase of carnations. While bride and bridegroom stood to attention she delivered a homily about the Executive Committee of the Soviet Working People. Then she handed two plain gold wedding rings to them. They exchanged rings; they were married. After another lecture, this time more domestic, Mr and Mrs Williams left her presence to the strains of *When the Saints Come Marching In*.

By far the most exhilarating visitor to the city was the British Foreign Secretary, Mr (now Lord) George Brown.

George — no journalist ever called him Mr Brown — had for some time been pumping fresh air into the corridors of the Foreign Office, disturbing clerks during their elevenses and ruffling diplomats becalmed during afternoon tea and biscuits.

It was therefore with some trepidation that the British Embassy in Moscow awaited the arrival of this adroit, sparrow-bright politician who had never sailed under the flagship Diplomacy. Their concern was fully justified.

George opened his innings by lambasting Embassy officials for allowing files to be handed out without any record of their withdrawal. He followed this up by commenting unfavourably on the check suit worn by one of the staff manning the reception desk. "That's a lovely weekend suit," he remarked, implying that it was hardly the thing for weekdays. His remark provoked bitterness from the Civil Service Union in London. Said a spokesman plaintively: "These men have to provide their own clothes."

The visit of Mr Anthony Wedgwood Benn was memorable only by comparison. It was so dull that it passed almost unnoticed. But it must be difficult for any left winger, more astute than the average run of blinkered politicians who visited the capital, to be ebullient when surrounded by evidence of the failure of the principles he has preached for so long.

* * *

The spectacular departure during the last phase of winter was the defection of Joseph Stalin's daughter, Svetlana, who sought political asylum in the United States.

The news was broken to me on the telephone by an excited David English. "Interview her son," he commanded. "Go, go, go," generating both enthusiasm and despair because such missions weren't that easy in Moscow.

Where, in the first place, did her son live? And what would be the attitude of the militia or KGB to an English journalist battering on the door of their Iron Dictator's progeny?

I telephoned Vladimir at Novosti and, after a brooding silence, he told me to await his call. It came surprisingly quickly. Svetlana's son, Joseph Morozov, he told me, lived in Flat 179 on the fourth floor of an apartment block facing the Kremlin across the Moscow River. Svetlana had also lived there with her third husband, an Indian Communist. I knocked on the door expecting nothing more dramatic than a bullet in the back and was relieved when, with Dima, I was invited indoors by Morozov, a twenty-two year-old medical student.

Joseph, a glossy-haired young man, didn't say anything of any great moment. He could hardly believe that his mother had defected, and added, "Let us say that her temperament was not even."

But the very fact that he had spoken at any length to a Western correspondent was significant and the interview made the front page lead in the *Express* the following day.

There was little doubt that I had been allowed to see Morozov because he was stoutly pro-Kremlin, because he cast doubts on his mother's state of mind and because his transparent bewilderment might persuade her to return home.

No matter. It was a hard news story and it served its purpose to inject a little of the Soviet viewpoint into a wealth of pro-West propaganda; in other words to help to project a balanced story, the avowed aim of every newspaper editor in a democratic climate.

VIII

Diplomats apart, the two most numerous breeds of foreigners in Moscow were defectors and journalists.

The defectors were known as the Twilight Brigade, shadowy, guilt-ridden figures inhabiting a No Man's Land between the Russian lines and the Western ghettos. With the exception of Len Wincott who had at least left his homeland with a flourish — and ironically been savagely punished by his mentors — they made only token attempts to mix socially, ashamed perhaps of the lacklustre existences into which their defections had deposited them.

They lived in utility flats boxed in gloomy apartment blocks, they worked mostly as translators in publishing houses and magazine offices and they kept company more with the bottle than each other.

I would have felt more sympathy for them if I had believed that they had defected for genuine idealistic reasons. But in most cases I suspected that their motives had been more self-important; that they had betrayed a society in which they felt they were unable to thrive, and exchanged it for transient notoriety and promises of privilege.

The Russians kept their word about the rewards. But who loves a traitor? The result was that they spent lives of unrelieved drabness unloved either by the Russians or their erstwhile compatriots.

Nor did I ever fully believe that even the leaders of the Twilight Brigade, men such as Guy Burgess, who had already drunk himself to death by the time I arrived in Moscow, Donald Maclean and Kim Philby, had been moved by idealism to commit their treachery. Their characters were so shifty, their justifications so glib, their morals so shallow, that it was impossible to associate them with any doctrine of universal equality.

I didn't meet any of the more notorious defectors, but, in the interests of my burgeoning novel, I did spend some time with some of the lesser turncoats.

One of them had been born in Australia, surely an unlikely country from which to defect. He was an elderly man with a grizzled, outdoor face and an accent as Australian as Foster's lager. Perhaps he had defected in protest at bodyline bowling!

We met in one of the dollar shops and he invited me to his apartment. Beneath his topcoat he was wearing a green suit and a crumpled grey pullover. He asked me if I wanted a beer, as if there were no other drink, and handed me a bottle of Russian beer, the glass of the brown bottle fluted like barley sugar.

He offered me a Russian cigarette, yellowish with a cardboard filter, and when I refused lit one himself, inhaling deeply and coughing shellbursts of smoke across the room. When the coughing had subsided he said: "So, you want to know why I did it?" I nodded, glancing around the small room at the crude furniture oozing with resin, at the worn carpet and the photographs of his family, frozen in time, on the mantelpiece.

"To tell you the truth," he said, "I don't know — it was a hell of a long time ago."

"But you must know what belief consigned you to this," gesturing at the shabby adornments of his *cell*.

"I just wanted to be someone, I guess. I was a seaman, you see. A nobody."

"And you became a somebody?"

"In my own mind I did. For a little while. Then I wanted to go back but it was too late."

"How long ago was that?"

"Twenty years ago, I guess."

"And you've regretted it ever since?"

"I wouldn't say that. They've been good to me in their own way. You see," he explained, "I always was a loner. That way you can live as an outcast."

"But what had you got to offer the Russians when you defected?"

"They didn't seem to want much. They interviewed me, put me on the radio . . . Do you know what I think it was?"

I shook my head. "I was the only Australian they had in their bag at that time."

"And you've actually been happy here?"

"As happy as I would be anywhere."

He was, I realised, telling the truth; he was that rare species, an honest defector. Apart from that single brain-storm when he had decided to be a somebody he had settled for mediocrity.

We finished our beer and I promised to visit him again. When I returned three months later he was dead. He had, I was told, died in his sleep. Alone.

One second-eleven defector whom I met at a dismal party thrown by the Soviet Foreign Ministry did manage to perk up my own national pride.

He was an Englishman whom I shall call Richard, a pale, sandy-haired academic whose defection eight years earlier had not agitated a single ripple of interest. He invited me to his barrack-block apartment, carpeted with worn rugs and scattered with books, where he lived with his Russian wife, a fragile, bespectacled girl who glided around the cramped rooms apparently deep in transcendental meditation.

The prospects for the afternoon seemed to be less than

titillating until Richard mentioned that he socialised with such infamous traitors as Philby and Maclean.

"Poor old Philby," he said as his wife disappeared into the kitchen to make tea.

"Poor?" I questioned. "Surely he should be euphoric. He plotted all his life in the interests of Communism. Now he's retired to enjoy its fruits — even if they are bitter lemons," I added.

"I didn't mean poor in that sense. I mean poor because he was duped."

I leaned forward in my chair. "Surely it was the British who were duped."

"Do you really believe that?"

I didn't want to, never had. From what I had read Philby had been suspected of being a spy and to allow him to continue to operate high up in the hierarchy of Intelligence had always seemed to be unbelievably naïve. What had happened to *Albion perfide*?

Richard's wife came in and poured us two cups of tea with lemon, offered a tin of sugar-crusted biscuits and departed to another room to consider matters more spiritual than espionage. Richard bit into his biscuit. "No," he said, "I think poor old Kim was used by the British. Fed whopping great lies which he passed onto the Kremlin. Red Herrings . . ." He smiled wanly.

"But surely he was a high-ranking officer in British Intelligence?"

"It's always easier to deceive the head of a department than an underling. The classic example, of course, is the intelligence organisation that bamboozles its own government."

"Has Philby told you this?"

He looked at me warily, the endemic expression of the defector in Moscow. A lock of sandy hair fell across his forehead, he sipped his tea. Finally he said: "You must understand my position." He put down his cup of tea and tightened the frayed knot of a striped tie, pennant of some distant college on which he had forever turned his back. "I am merely telling you what I have inferred."

"What about Burgess and Maclean?"

"I think the same applied to them. Can the British really have been so fatuous in their attitude to Burgess? No one, but no one, allows a drunken homosexual to operate with impunity when he has access to confidential information. They use him, my dear fellow, that's what they do."

I knew that there was no chance that he would confirm that either Philby or Maclean had reluctantly come to the conclusion that they had been outwitted, victims of a triple cross. But I was left with the impression that Richard wasn't merely making inferences: he had been told.

Heady stuff. Especially in light of subsequent assertions about Anthony Blunt, one-time Adviser for the Queen's Pictures and Drawings, and allegations about Sir Roger Hollis, head of M15 from 1956 to 1965.

Perhaps we had, in fact, been positively perfidious instead of calamitously credulous.

*　　*　　*

Of the foreign journalists outside my circle it was the Swedes who enjoyed themselves the most. They imported pretty wives, they made their apartments neat and snug and burned sculptured candles in them, they loved the snow and ice and treated surveillance with scant respect.

One of them was particularly cavalier in his attitude. As he was also accident prone, his contributions to expatriate life were often spectacular. Shortly after his arrival he learned from some undisclosed source that the Minister of Defence, Marshall Grechko, had died. Unaware that this rumour surfaced every week he immediately called his office in Stockholm and dictated what he considered to be a baptisimal exclusive. The following day he saw the good marshal on Red Square but appeared to be unperturbed at the reincarnation. "Never mind," he said, "he's got to go one day and you can't deny that I was first with the story."

He then entered enthusiastically into the winter sport scene and, on his first day on skates, plunged into a basement area and broke his leg.

The least extrovert were the Americans and West Germans, understandably because they were the fall guys. The Germans were stigmatised by World War II, the Americans by Vietnam. Antagonism between the Russians and these two nationalities had for many years been underlined by various surveillance incidents.

In 1964 the Germans had discovered that, not only was their embassy conventionally bugged, but the Russians had managed to fit an electronic gadget to a teletype and were reading secret messages to Bonn as they were dispatched. At about the same time a Russian defector to the West revealed to the Americans the locations of more than forty bugs hidden in the walls of their embassy.

It was therefore not surprising that the Americans largely kept their own counsel and that a West German correspondent in a flat above me spent most of his leisure hours listening to hi-fi with earphones as big as saucers clamped to his head.

The Japanese were gregarious, at the same time working with an industry that put many of us to shame; the Italians were thin on the ground; the French were personified by a reporter named Jean-Pierre who wore red braces and endeared himself to party hostesses by kissing the arms of female guests from wrist to elbow.

But the most intriguing representative of a foreign newspaper was Victor Louis of the London *Evening News*, the man I had met on my arrival in Moscow. This slim, wavy-haired Russian had worked in a minor capacity at both the New Zealand and Brazilian Embassies in Moscow before being arrested and sent to a labour camp for dealing on the black market. In the camp he was apparently employed as an *agent provocateur* persuading dissidents to talk freely.

On his release he mixed freely with Westerners in Moscow and, according to a KGB major, Yuri Nosenko, who defected to the west, he worked for the Moscow district of the secret police. By the time I met him it was believed that he had risen higher in the KGB hierarchy.

His job was disinformation and propaganda and he zealously pursued his calling from his luxurious dacha where he lived with his wife, an attractive girl from Surrey. He was a frequent visitor to my apartment where he ate and drank frugally and in his soft voice dispensed what have since come to be known as "inspired leaks".

One such leak was the return to Russia of Mrs Julia Finklestein whose husband Leonid, a scientific journalist, had been granted asylum in London. The Soviet Premier, Alexei Kosygin, had granted her a re-entry visa into Russia; he had also indicated that she could return to her husband.

Mrs Finklestein duly went back to Britain and it wasn't until a few months later that Victor Louis again raised the subject.

"Do you remember your first paragraph on that story?" he asked.

I shook my head.

"It said that Mrs Finklestein faced an agonising choice: husband or country."

"And?"

"She's chosen country," said Victor, purring over his cup of tea.

It was a typical Louis operation and that day I was able to interview the defector's wife who told me that she had discovered that her husband had been planning to leave her for years.

"I just couldn't bear the deceit," she told me.

Louis was delighted with the story because he had effectively countered the anti-Soviet propaganda surrounding the husband's departure. That was his job and, however vehemently Westerners reviled him, he was good at it.

So much so that he was allowed to travel the world in luxurious style and managed to obtain an invitation to the White House to meet the then Vice-President, Hubert H. Humphrey.

*   *   *

The foreigners who faced the greatest challenge in Moscow were the women. While their menfolk were pursuing their professions they had to find ways to fill their leisure hours in an alien city.

Most of them employed maids so there was no escape in housework or cooking. Instead they plunged enthusiastically into a variety of wildly diversified occupations.

The one common experience was Russian lessons which were given in their apartments by Soviet tutors. Considerately, the UPKD provided teachers exuding masculinity and women freshly arrived in the city were warned by embassy officials to be wary of linguistic Lotharios.

Some wives went skating or skiing on the Lenin Hills, the gentle slopes equipped with a ski-jump overlooking Moscow; others attended ballet, keep-fit and cooking lessons. One group of Americans gathered once a week to sing madrigals. Mostly the women coped triumphantly although one or two had to be flown home on the brink of nervous breakdowns.

Diane seemed to find no difficulty in occupying herself. She complained, in fact, that a twenty-four hour day was too

101

short. When she wasn't supervising Valentina, teaching Dima French or doing battle with the shopkeepers she was painting and sketching. For hours she disappeared in the city to return, cherry-nosed and triumphant, with a pad full of charcoal drawings — churches, Kremlin towers, market scenes, old men fishing through holes in the frozen river.

When she heard that the Kremlin was to permit an exhibition of avant-garde paintings — a complete reversal of their policy towards the arts — she reacted excitedly. We were unable to attend on the first day because I was covering a conference. On the second day we presented ourselves at the entrance to the gallery — and were informed coldly that the police had closed down the exhibition. Why? Because it was decadent, of course. We shrugged and returned to the apartment to pursue our own variations of decadence.

For single girls the problems were equally pressing but far more delectable, namely a surfeit of admirers in the foreign community. Mostly embassy secretaries or nannies, they were surrounded at cocktail parties by men as thick as aphides on a leaf; as they placed unlit cigarettes between their lips half a dozen lighters flamed simultaneously. At the dances at the American and British clubs they were obliged to hoof it all night and, when they went to collect their coats, were faced by platoons of panting, prospective escorts.

They were also prime targets for more sinister suitors — charming and handsome young Russians, or diplomats from Communist countries, who sought not only their bodies but their souls. The more attractive girls, already well versed in masculine wiles, had no difficulty in repelling the pests; but less worldly women were often confused by sudden concentrated courtship.

All had been warned that, as a matter of course, the KGB would try and recruit them to steal secret information from their employers. But the approaches were not always that obvious. Picture a middle-aged spinster who meets a Russian of about the same age, attractive but far too ordinary to be a gigolo, in an art gallery. Subsequently, over coffee, she learns that, far from being a KGB agent, he detests the secret police and has suffered at their hands.

Just such a woman working in a West European embassy was approached in this way that winter. She shared with her attentive new friend a love of paintings, particularly icons, and listened sympathetically to his stories of persecution by the KGB. He was vague about the crime that had merited this attention but prophesied that, if he were ever again accused of even the slightest demeanour, he would be thrown into a labour camp for at least ten years.

The woman didn't tell her superiors about this friendship because they wouldn't understand how innocent it was. And when the friend suggested that they make love in his apartment she didn't demur because it was merely the sealing of companionship founded on compassion and loneliness.

The photographs shown to her by a KGB officer two days later, however, showed that the love-making had far exceeded anything that could reasonably be described as token coupling.

The KGB, said the officer, were contemplating arresting her friend on a morals charge and, as he had a previous record, he would probably be sent to a camp for the rest of his life. But, if she agreed to co-operate with them in certain matters, there was every chance that her lover would be saved from such a fate.

Happily for her embassy, the woman was sensible enough to appreciate what she had probably subconsciously suspected all along: that her friend was an agent rather than a victim of the KGB and that she had been set up from the moment she met him in the art gallery.

She reported what had happened to her own people and was

posted to an embassy in South America. It seemed to me infinitely sad that, in the interests of espionage, the emotions of such a woman, stored like pressed flowers, should callously have been re-awoken.

And it wasn't until several years later that I learned that in South America she had married a man half her age.

IX

Entertainment and recreation were never lacking in Moscow and one bitterly cold day Gilbert Lewthwaite and I decided to add sub-zero swimming to our experiences. We pulled the flaps of our fur hats over our ears — if we hadn't we might have lost them — and set off for the pool in Gilbert's new red Moskvich.

It was so cold that, while I waited outside the pool for Gilbert to remove the windscreen-wipers, the cigar-butt between my fingers froze into a bullet of ice. Inside the chlorine-smelling entrance to the pool a beefy woman attendant issued us with tickets and directed us into the interior.

Did I for a moment detect compassion in her gaze? Did anyone ever return after she had dispatched them into the armoury of steel lockers ahead? Or were we wheeled out, frozen cadavers to be slipped deftly into the morgue?

When we reached the lockers another large woman in white planted herself in front of us. She handed us each a scrubbing-brush, a cake of carbolic soap — and a blue bathing cap.

"*Niet,*" I said. "*Niet, niet, niet,*" waving the bathing cap. And to Gilbert: "I'm not going through with it."

"Too bad old man," said Gilbert, his North Country vowels sharpened by the cold. "I'm going to write a feature about it."

"Well I'm not wearing this," brandishing the bathing cap

like a wife who has found another woman's brassiere in her husband's pocket.

"Please yourself," said Gilbert. "Personally I think it will suit you."

"*Niet.*" I shook my head fiercely at the woman in white.

"*Da.*" She gave me a shove that propelled me towards the lockers. "*Da, da, da.*"

We took off our coats and fur hats and hung them in the lockers. Then shoes, socks, jackets, waistcoats. The woman, her black hair combed into a bun, stood, arms akimbo, gazing menacingly at us.

Gilbert shrugged and slipped out of his underpants and into his swimming trunks in one oiled movement. He then regarded me with the patronising air of a man who has performed such an operation countless times while I groped around inside an inadequate towel tied round my stomach.

Exuding an air of modest achievement, we made our way to the entrance to the pool. There we were stopped by a second woman in white.

She pointed at my crotch.

"My God," I said, "what does she want?"

"What do you think she wants," Gilbert said. "She obviously fancies you."

The attendant swung her finger in the direction of Gilbert's trunks, balled her fist and made energetically suggestive movements. Gilbert, features contorted with horror, said: "I'm getting out of here."

She snatched his scrubbing-brush from his hand. More violent movements. Apparently she wanted us to remove our trunks and give our parts a good old-fashioned lathering.

I tried to make a run for it but an iron arm barred my way.

"Nothing for it, old man," said Gilbert.

We took off our trunks and scrubbed ourselves while she stared at us impassively.

106

At last we reached the entrance to the pool and, afraid of renewing the wardress's wrath, put on our bathing caps. We looked as incongruous as two astronauts on the London Underground.

But the ordeal was far from over. To reach the pool you had to swim through a steaming tunnel. Suffocation, drowning or heart failure induced by fear — you took your choice.

We dived in and emerged in the huge pool, blue-capped heads bobbing like corks. High above snow was falling, but it melted as it reached the cocoon of steam enveloping the pool. The water was warm and buoyant and we swam like dolphins.

But the steam and the bathing caps played strange tricks. On entering the pool I had noticed a pretty girl from the British Embassy swimming about in her blue cap. By now thoroughly skittish I swam up behind a blue-capped figure, gave the waist in front of me a little squeeze and said: "We've got to stop meeting like this."

The figure turned round and I stared deep into the dismayed brown eyes of a Middle East ambassador.

Other relaxations were more conventional. But for me one was quite unconventional. Ballet.

In Fleet Street I had belonged to that school of hard-news reporters whose recreations consisted traditionally of drinking reservoirs of beer and watching Westerns on television. And so it was with a faint feeling of shame that I succumbed to the blandishments of the Bolshoi, its regally sumptuous setting and its vibrant atmosphere.

I was finally cleansed of my guilt when I studied the audience: with their open-necked white shirts and winter toughened features they looked about as aesthetic as the All Blacks rugby team. In fact they were highly critical devotees and they could destroy a production. A mere two curtain calls and a ballerina could start thinking about retirement.

Tickets were difficult to obtain unless you were privileged

— Dima merely had to pick up the 'phone to get a couple — and ticket touts operated in the shadows of the theatre's massive portals. When the doors opened it was like the rush-hour at Charing Cross station. Once inside the atmosphere closed in and when the curtain rose in the red and gold auditorium the faces of these bulldozing men and their sturdy wives were touched with grace.

Because of an arrangement between the *Express* and the Russian agency Novosti, I was one of the few Western journalists allowed behind the scenes of the Bolshoi.

While massive-thighed men leapt around I interviewed an up-and-coming dancer named Natasha Bessmertnova. She was a slight, fragile-boned little thing and her name meant 'Immortal'. She told me: "My favourite ballet is Giselle. It is all about love and that is what ballet is all about."

When I returned to London on holiday I told one of my colleagues not renowned for his artistic appreciation that I had interviewed a ballet dancer. "Lucky sod," he said. "I saw one in Cairo once but she put me off my dinner."

*   *   *

We visited the circus and the cinema and we went to pubs which we found outside the confines of Intourist Moscow. They were big sweating places, rather like the pubs round Victoria Station; they served foaming glasses of beer and plates of crustacea and I never understood why they were kept from tourists. Perhaps they were too reminiscent of Dickensian London.

It was this sort of class-conscious logic that made the Russians bar great tracts of their land from foreigners. Foreign military attachés would pore over their maps debating some massive deployment of troops when the real culprit was a shabby village in need of a lick of paint.

Correspondents had to apply for permission to visit anywhere outside a radius of thirty miles or so of Moscow. The sterner critics of the Soviet regime found this sinister; they tended to forget that similar rules applied to Russian journalists in London.

This restriction was waived on the route to Zavidovo, a country retreat on the Volga where foreigners could spend a few days in one of the dachas borrowed from the pages of *War and Peace*. Diane and I spent New Year's Eve there with Gilbert Lewthwaite and John Miller and their wives.

As soon as we reached the countryside winter changed its coat; there were shadows in the hollows in the snow and the late afternoon sun shone as though through stained-glass windows and peace settled on the fields.

At the dacha we skated and I tried to ski with cross-country skis fashioned like floorboards. We played the Russian version of Pool, we ate sausages and kippers imported from England and we sang *Auld Lang Syne* as the snow fell prettily in the lamplight outside the windows.

When we got back to Moscow it was still bleak. Soiled snow covered the rooftops and I noticed that whereas country people faced the cold with their chests thrust out city dwellers ducked into it, butting it angrily with their heads.

In the evenings we continued to adjourn to the American Club on the other side of the city or the British Club below the apartment. British nannies employed by diplomats favoured the American Club hoping, as their mothers had hoped in World War II, to marry an oil-rich Texan.

Drinks at the American Club were stronger, the movies slicker, the jiving more spectacular. But the likes of John Miller, Gilbert and myself preferred the British Club; the English beer was warmer, the movies more homely and you could always let yourself go with an abandoned Palais Glide or a decadent Hokey-Cokey.

The British Club was really a glorious cliché. Identical institutions, largely unaffected by climate or custom, exist all over the world. The conversation — language, servants, the weather in the United Kingdom and the Test Match score — is the same and locals are received under sufferance because, although they may well be citizens of the host country, they are after all foreigners.

Bingo and darts were two of the biggest attractions in the Moscow premises. After the last pint of tepid beer and the last Old Fashioned Waltz, we used to emerge into the Moscow night with a sense of shock. Shouldn't we have been in Bromley?

Eventually the Russians closed down both clubs because, they said, the premises were needed for other purposes. But I always suspected that a contributory reason was the choice of films at the British Club. Was it really necessary to screen a movie exploring in detail the Soviet espionage organisation in Britain?

X

It would be impossible in the West to be in almost daily contact with someone without *getting to know them*. Not in Russia. But I was determined that neither Vladimir, Dima, nor Valentina should be blank pages in my scrapbook; and so, like an ornithologist keeping watch on a protected species, I observed them, compiling personalities from their habits and from occasional glimpses through holes in the fences erected around them to keep out foreigners.

Through this furtive performance I hoped, also, to spy on the Soviet character denuded of its uniform. But not — heaven forbid! — to try and compose a National Character because that would have been absurd in a land ninety times the size of the United Kingdom inhabited by Russians, Ukrainians, Tartars, Armenians, Georgians . . .

Valentina didn't pose as many problems as Vladimir and Dima. She was peasant stock, only better fed tham most. Not that *peasant* immediately filed her away; but it did provide a foundation for scrutiny.

With centuries of penury behind her, she was a great improviser and provider: within an hour a bag of bones became a stew and whatever we left on our plates soon sizzled appetisingly in the kitchen. She would have revelled in Spanish *paella* said to have evolved from hard times. She wasn't enamoured with housework but she applied herself to the chores with a trance-like industry that I recognised having laboured in the RAF in a similar somnambulistic state.

She could be joyous, carrot-red hair and cheeks aflame, and fill the apartment with song; she could be soulful, the Russian euphemism for moody, particularly if Diane had plucked up courage to reprimand her. When such a mood was upon her she breathed so heavily, sighed so brokenly, that she infected the whole place with her melancholy and we had to flee.

She was, like most Russians, superstitious, but whereas most of them played it down she positively quivered with it. If I shook hands with a visitor on the threshold of the apartment she squealed with dismay because it was the prelude to conflict; if I whistled indoors — and I have always been an enthusiastic if unmelodious whistler — she would clamp her hands to her ears because I was summoning bad luck. A bird, thank God, never flew through the open window: it is a portent of death.

Being superstitious myself I respected this concern with the omens but thought that some Russians took it to extremes: to cement good fortune in the West we say, "Touch wood" — in the Soviet Union they spit over their shoulders. If you happen to be standing behind them the good fortune is open to question.

In common with most Muscovites Valentina took to the Great Outdoors on every possible occasion, travelling by bus with friends and family to the fringes of the city and tramping through forests of pine and birch carpeted with snow; and, when the snow had melted, foraging for herbs and berries with which to ginger-up her bubbling stews.

I always felt that she should have lived in a village of pink or blue-painted wooden houses built around a parish pump. In the countryside her appetites would have found more natural outlets and her abundant presence would have been honed by the exigencies of winter and the industries of summer.

112

Vladimir, too, was an outdoor man; but his restraints, I sensed, were more political than urban. He was utterly loyal to the system but that is not to say that sometimes beneath the trappings of doctrinaire the call of the wild wasn't heard, the spring summons to the hibernating animal.

Yet if Vladimir was a hunter he was a sophisticated one; that breed that likes to round off a predatory day in the bush with a dry martini, a good dinner and a soft bed. He had a house somewhere on the edge of Moscow, a good wife — that much he confided — and children brought up to enjoy breathing fresh air.

His professional mantle, selling politics and deadly dull ones at that, seemed to contradict all this open-plan living. But I suppose that, like ninety per cent of mankind, he adapted.

Our conversations, when we were not arguing explosively about blood sports, sometimes touched upon Communism and Capitalism, but on this subject we veered sharply away from each other like two ornamental fish in a tank. I admired his allegiance to the system he served because he had lived in America, and had enjoyed its luxuries and its freedoms. On the other hand he had returned to a country where you could still walk the streets without fear of being shot, where there was no concentration of ghetto poverty.

Sometimes, as the good Georgian wine settled in our bellies and the smoke of the bad Cuban cigars hung between us, it occurred to me that perhaps we avoided direct confrontation because we were both overly sensitive about the imperfections of the societies we had been born into: that it was pointless to embark on an argument in which neither of us truly believed: that each had settled for the best of two evils. Or was it the worst? To put it more simply, we understood each other, this sleek, heavily-built, quick-witted KGB agent and myself.

Of the three of them Dima was by far the most difficult to evaluate because, devotion to the AS apart, he was the most introverted. When you tried to peer into his soul you were diverted by a flash of light on his gold-rimmed spectacles or a nervous flutter of his hands.

He was married to a pretty, dark-haired girl — the description necessarily scanty because the photograph he showed me had been taken with a camera held in a trembling hand. No mention was made of any children. He was a sensitive young man with an inquiring mind, but his sensibilities took a terrible battering situated as he was in a Capitalist outpost in the capital of Socialism. How could he equate the relative luxuries of our life with the bleak realities of his own? How could he explain to himself the vitality that leaped from British newspapers and magazines when he was daily submerged in the mire of Soviet editorial platitudes?

To survive such comparisons you had to possess great spiritual fortitude, and I believe Dima possessed just such defences, sustained (and I was only just beginning to realise that this applied to most Russians) by a force far more emotive than Party allegiance — patriotism.

On only a few occasions did I ever manage to raise such delicate matters, and always when we were out walking. My offensive stemmed from two unsubtle but valid questions: *How could a people of such passionate, romantic and courageous temperament have allowed themselves to fall into the hands of such grey, implacable masters? How could anyone put up with a system that had manifestly failed?*

Off would come Dima's glasses for a thorough polish while face intense beneath his woollen hat, he would consider his defence. Then, breath smoking on the cold air as we tramped through Gorky Park or marched briskly past the mounting skyscrapers of Kalinin Prospect, he would deliver packaged answers to the two questions.

"But, Derek, we do not accept that the system has failed. What you don't understand is that before the Revolution we had nothing. Now, by comparison, we have everything."

"But, Dima, that was fifty years ago. Surely you have a right to expect more than a bed of flints after half a century."

"But we had —"

"I know, Dima, you had a war in which you lost twenty million. They were probably the most terrible losses ever inflicted on one nation and the world grieved for you. But that was twenty-three years ago . . ."

"And when you talk about romanticism, our heritage, all that, you must realise that, before the Revolution, only the rich could indulge in such fancies. The peasants had courage all right: that was all they were permitted."

"But none of this explains the shortages, the queues, the shoddy goods, the cramped accommodation . . ." And, I wanted to add, the repression that consigned any dissenter to a labour camp, but I refrained because Dima was himself a minute part (and an unlikely one at that) of that apparatus.

Off would come the spectacles for another polish with the end of his scarf. Then, glancing perhaps with deserved pride at the Ostankino TV tower which stands like a giant lance embedded beside Moscow's outer ring road, he would embark on another earnest explanation.

"You talk about inferior products, bad accommodation . . . What are such deprivations compared with the evils in the West — violence, pollution, racism, pornography . . ."

"But at least they're out in the open, not suppressed as they are in the Soviet Union."

"Does that make them any better?"

"No," I said conceding the point, "but I don't accept that none of these evils exist over here. You just don't read about them, that's all."

"But that is a different argument altogether. We believe that to publicise such matters only encourages people to indulge in them."

"With respect, Dima," I said firmly, "that's hypocritical rubbish. The Soviet press has no hesitation in publicising drunkeness, laziness or corruption. Why? To remind people of the penalties, that's why. To deter them. What they don't broadcast are the imperfections of society that reflect adversely on the government."

Adroitly discarding this card, Dima would ask: "Why do you always concentrate on these aspects? Why don't you consider our achievements? In space, for instance."

"But at what cost? Surely it would have been preferable to build another million houses than to win the space race?"

And Dima would shake his head emphatically. "The people have to have heroes."

"And homes!"

"Do you see any unhappy children in Moscow?"

"I don't see many unhappy children in the West."

And so it would go on, as inconclusive as a cruise-ship romance, until we reached home to be silenced, gratefully, by the omnipresent eavesdroppers.

At the end of my sojourn in the Soviet Union I was able to paste sketches, no more, of Vladimir, Dima and Valentina in my scrapbook. Predictably I hadn't got much nearer to the soul of the Russian people.

What I did know was that it had lost none of its poetry, its torment, its epic passions: it was merely that fate had wrapped it in grey packaging. But whereas the soul is durable packaging is not.

*　　*　　*

In an atmosphere where contact between foreigners and Soviet citizenry was discouraged it was difficult to make contacts outside your pre-selected circle. But on holiday beside the sea it was easier.

To escape briefly from the mailed fist of winter Diane and I flew south for a long weekend at Sochi on the Black Sea, a resort kneeling at the altar of the Caucasus Mountains in obeisance to the local god HEALTH.

Leave Sochi in bad health at your peril. It is not so much a town as Harley-Street-By-The-Sea. A chain, a hundred miles or so long, of spas, solariums, clinics, sanitoriums and rest-homes. You converse over a glass of mineral water not about politics or the cost-of-living or sex but about blood pressure, migraines or, most titillating of all, unidentified maladies. For hypochondriacs it is Mecca. And its temple is a centre called Matsesta where you can take the waters to treat heart disorders, skin diseases, hypertension, neuroses . . . if you suffered from constipation you'd probably get a run for your money! Every year five hundred thousand make the pilgrimage in search of the grail of health as though the blue waters of the Black Sea were one vast reservoir of patent medicine.

We arrived in February and already Soviet germs were in full retreat across the sea to Turkey. Chests swelling, cheeks glowing, the healthy strode the esplanade with its flights of white steps and pergolas, paddled in the waves or swam in warm, sea-water baths.

The forest, speared with cypress, swept right down to the shore and, in places, vaulted the railway lines, more lakeside than seaside. Behind, vanishing into drooping cloud, the Caucasus and snow-capped Elbrus (18,510 feet), Europe's highest mountain. Hydrofoils skimmed the waters, helicopters buzzed over the mountains. We breathed the bright air and felt better immediately. Not only were germs on the run but dark spectres of repression had been sent packing.

This was the Russia of which you rarely read. Clouds high and free over the crumpled mountains, music strumming the nights, Russians who spoke to you without glancing over their shoulders. We walked up a mountain road to Dagomys, capital of Russian tea, and drank a brew with a Kuban pie in a log cabin; we drove to a grove fifteen miles from the centre of Sochi to survey yew and box trees eight hundred years old; we ate trout caught in a hatchery silent with deep mossy water.

On the third day, after politely declining an invitation to visit the N Ostrovsky Memorial Museum on the grounds that I had never heard of N Ostrovsky, I decided to do something healthy. I would have settled for a draught of some Caucasian elixir but Diane insisted that I immerse myself in a more salubrious pastime.

So I had a bath.

The *banya*, or bathhouse, is as Russian as a pub is British. And it was here, breathing steam instead of swallowing bitter, that I met a contact who most certainly wasn't a plant.

Entrance to the bathhouse cost the equivalent of forty pence, the price including a rough towel with which to drape yourself and a bundle of birch twigs with which to beat the dirt out of your skin — or the skin of any neighbouring masochist. We sat in our towels in a gloomy torture chamber snouting with pipes and tiered with wooden steps. From the pipes issued steam, soft and scented and sinister.

The heat wrinkled the skin, seared the eyeballs, took off you ears if you weren't careful. The higher the tier the hotter the steam; I crouched on the bottom rung while, above me, exuberant Russians thrashed themselves and their friends and debated their cures.

Having decided that I was done to a turn I was about to leave the *banya* when I felt a tap on the shoulder. I wheeled round to see a plump little man beaming at me through a mask of sweat.

He indicated his back and spoke to me in Russian. I told him that I couldn't speak Russian; the smile broadened and he said in immaculate English: "My back, could you give it a few strokes, please."

Flagellation had never been my preference. However, if you can't join them, beat them. He lowered his towel to his waist and I gave him a few half-hearted blows reflecting that a photograph of the scene was the best blackmail material the KGB could have hoped for.

"Harder," he said.

I administered a few more desultory strokes while somewhere amid the billowing clouds a sado-masochist poured more water on the hot bricks making the pipes steam like dragons' nostrils.

"That's fine," he said. "Fancy a beer?"

I blinked my scalding eyelids. The heat had got to me. Any minute now he would put on his bowler, pick up his brolly and walk out into Ludgate Circus.

"Outside in the changing room," he said. "The attendant will get us some. I think you've had just about enough of this if you're not used to it."

In the changing room the saloon-bar bonhomie continued as the bathers cooled off, drank beer and chewed salt fish as hard as shoe-leather.

"My name's Mikhail," said the plump little man. "I come here from Moscow twice a year to get rid of some of this," sadly squeezing a roll of flesh around his midriff. "But as soon as I get back to the city I put it back on."

"This doesn't help, does it?" I asked as the attendant brought two mugs of beer.

"Oh but you have to drink your beer," he said, swallowing some and smacking his lips. "It's part of the ritual."

"Does it really do any good?"

He shrugged. "It gets you away from your wife."

His wife turned out to be as plump and jolly as her husband. While he had been in the *banya* she, too, had been sweating off the pounds in an adjoining bathhouse.

We all met that evening in a restaurant built like an old mill where we ate cutlets and drank rich red wine.

"So," she said, "what did you think of our little relaxation?"

119

"If that's your relaxation," I said, "I shouldn't like to endure any of your hardship."

She laughed — they both laughed hugely as though merriment was bottled inside them — and said: "It's the Russian way. What we enjoy most of all is getting out of the damned places."

Diane asked them where they had learned such fluent and easy English and Mikhail told us that he had worked for Intourist, the Soviet travel agency, in various European capitals.

"And do you know the place we like best?" his wife asked. "Sochi?"

"Damn right," said Mikhail.

We met them a couple more times, weighing a little less on each occasion, and they talked sensibly about the rights and wrongs of life in the Soviet Union. Especially about holidays.

"A family can come here for a whole month for as much as you would pay for a weekend in Brighton," Mikhail said. "So it can't be all that damn bad can it?"

They lived in an apartment near Arbatskaya Square in Moscow and I was overjoyed that I had at last struck up a friendship outside the appointed few. Three weeks after we returned to Moscow I called on Mikhail and his wife to see if they had replaced the lost flesh.

Mikhail opened the door; behind him stood another man whose features I couldn't make out.

I stuck out my hand. "So," I said, "how's my favourite weight-watcher?"

He stared through me. "I'm afraid I don't understand," he said.

"Mikhail, it's me, Derek."

"Derek?" He shook his head. "I know nobody of that name."

"But —"

"I'm sorry."
The door closed firmly on our friendship.

XI

In Russia women were granted equality with men many years ago. It was written into the Constitution in the thirties but really implemented after World War II because of the shortage of manpower.

But what equality! If Germaine Greer had championed Women's Lib Soviet style in the West she would have been lynched. The equality flourishes professionally, ends domestically. While the man puts his feet up after a hard day's labour the woman has to do her housework after an equally exhausting day's work.

Thus the divorce rate is high and family togetherness, always one of the hallowed facets of Russian society, is suffering — although old people still fare better than they do in the West.

Even the equality at work is suspect. The pay may be equal but if there's dirty work to be done — a ditch to be dug, a boiler to be cleaned — then the woman gets the job. Why does she put up with this unequal *equality*? Because she has no option: to make ends meet she has to supplement her husband's pay. But she can take advantage of certain dubious sops such as free abortion — legal long before it was in the West — and State nursery schools.

When I asked a woman at a party what birth control was practised she told me: "Abortion, fatigue and overcrowding."

And despite all this the Russian male still likes to assert his masculinity; in today's parlance he is macho. Drunkenness and infidelity are not openly condoned, but neither are they condemned out of hand.

An American correspondent employed a woman interpreter whose daughter had been unhappily married to an all-male male who used to beat her up when the fires of vodka were smouldering in his belly. When she had a baby and took her four-month paid maternity leave-of-absence from work he besported himself with other women from the factory where he worked. If she remonstrated she got a black eye.

When the child, a girl, was established in the State nursery and she was back at work she fell in love with a man who was both masculine *and* kind. But she didn't leave home because she cherished her small family unit and, perhaps, still harboured some threadbare affection for her husband.

When the husband found out about his rival he flew into a rage, knocked her about and started divorce proceedings. His wife was ostracised and he attracted much sympathy in their community.

*   *   *

Reluctantly I once accompanied Diane to a fashion show. I might, she argued, get some material for a feature.

What astonished me was the fragile elegance of the models. Russian women are not necessarily buxom, but nor are they sylph-like. To my inexpert eye the gowns might have been made by a Parisian couturier: to the women in the audience dressed in the austerity styles of 1939-45 they must have been magical.

I asked Dima what he thought of these lovely creatures wafting up and down the stage, posing hands on slender hips and he said: "Too skinny." According to Diane the dresses weren't at all bad, high praise from a girl raised in fashion-conscious Montreal.

But were these clothes really for sale? Or was I participating in some elaborate public relations exercise? At the end of the show there was a ripple of applause, the models retired to the hot-house where they had been nurtured and the women in the audience stormed a counter where, unbelievably, the fashions were said to be on sale.

Diane joined the scrum, shoving with the best of them, and disappeared from view.

When she emerged she was empty-handed.

"Well?" I said.

"They were for sale all right," she said.

"Why didn't you buy any then?"

"Because I'm not a dressmaker. All they're selling are the patterns."

*　　*　　*

But the deprivations endured by Soviet women are offset by many good things.

They can, for instance, take a long cheap holiday in the sun and scorch on the beaches of the Black Sea; they can spend weekends skiing or skating or walking through the silent forests; they can submerge themselves in culture — opera, ballet, music, theatre — making their sorties for a few pennies on buses, trams or by the immaculate underground. And, with the black-clad babushka (grandmother) always ready to baby-sit, they can have a night out with the girls every bit as tempestuous as their husbands'.

One night when I was dining with Diane in a Georgian restaurant I witnessed a knees-up involving a couple of dozen women from the professional classes. (About three quarters of Soviet doctors are women and every court I attended was

124

presided over by a woman.)

The food was being devoured with exuberant appreciation as was the vodka, wine and brandy. Towards the end of the meal they were feeling no pain at all. They hugged each other, administered friendly punches on the shoulder, laughed uproariously and, of course, sang. At first drinking songs, then marching songs and, then, because these revived the misery of war, songs as sad as tears.

Diane and I were invited to join the party and Diane was promptly assailed with questions about a woman's role in the West, the revellers delighted to find that she could speak passable Russian. With me they were less delighted: I was an interloper and I was inarticulate.

After a while a matronly lady who spoke English took pity on me. She poured me wine, gazed at me fondly and gave the impression that she was about to pick me up, press me to her formidable bosom and feed me from the bottle.

I asked her what work she did and she said: "First I am a housewife, second I am an architect. But please do not mis-understand me," refilling my glass, "I am proud to be both. A woman who is a housewife only is not fulfilling her duty to the motherland."

For a woman looking like a cartoonist's impression of a dowager duchess she was remarkably forthcoming about sex.

"Russian men," she said, "poof! They are selfish." She made a gesture with one hand which I took to mean a quick on/off operation. Her face softened. "But they *are* men. And what men!" leaving the impression that an immense amount was achieved between the on and the off.

"And what women!" I said gallantly.

"You like Russian woman?"

"Of course," shifting uncomfortably in my seat because this woman should have been taking tea after opening the vicarage fete, not drinking wine and discussing sex.

"We have great hearts," she said, thumping other great parts of her anatomy.

"Here's to Russian womanhood," I said, raising my glass.

"And to our men!"

"To Russia."

"To friendship."

"To love."

"Ah, to love." She kissed me on the cheek and whispered: "You should have married a Russian woman. She would have fixed you."

I didn't doubt it; but I decided to leave before any fixing was put into practise. I extricated Diane from a group of inquisitive women and we left as the gathering broke into a song of passionate intensity. Later, no doubt, a good many husbands were soundly fixed.

*   *   *

Some of the most attractive Russian girls were to be found behind the counters of the hard-currency *Beryozka* shops. There was about them a conspiratorial charm; they were selling luxury goods unavailable to the ordinary Russian, their customers were priviliged compatriots or decadent foreigners and they knew perfectly well that, quite innocently, they were party to black market deals.

Probably half of what was sold over their counters for pounds, dollars, marks or rouble coupons was resold illegally at anything up to ten times the price paid. So each shop assistant was a commercial Mata Hari, beckoning with a knowing smile from behind her merchandise — perfumes, amber necklaces, silks, caviar, imported clothes . . .

One of the girls in the *Beryozka* on Kutuzovsky Prospect was a stunning beauty. Shiny black hair in coils, almond-shaped eyes the colour of the sea, movements unconsciously provocative. She was selling me a necklace of Baltic amber, warm fossilised resin cupped in her hand, when an American correspondent whom I shall call Harry joined us.

Harry was a young man with glossy good looks, exuding good health and good intentions, who frequently derided correspondents who succumbed to the wiles of pretty girls employed by the KGB.

"Hallo, Harry," I said, taking the curled-up necklace from the girl. "How are things?"

No reply.

Harry was staring at the girl like a blind man whose sight has just been restored. She, too, was transfixed. I could feel the chemistry between them and I could have pocketed the necklace there and then and departed without paying for it.

Harry finally bought a set of beaming Russian dolls from the girl. She lowered her gaze, murmured a few words in English and went to serve another customer. At the door to the street I glanced round: those green eyes were fixed on Harry's retreating back.

Outside the shop Harry said: "Wow!"

"Forget it, Harry," I said. "Practise what you preach."

But he wasn't listening.

The following day he called at my apartment, a thing he'd never done before. "How about a walk?" he suggested, meaning a talk.

As we strode briskly over a bridge spanning the Moscow River he said suddenly: "I went back, you know."

"Harry," I said, glancing towards the gilded baubles of the Kremlin floating in a grey sky, "remember what you said about all those other correspondents that were caught."

"But those were all deliberate set-ups."

"This girl works for the State."

"But not for the KGB."

"How do you know? She probably reports back on all

127

Russians spending dollar coupons. In any case she could soon be enrolled."

"So what do you think I should do?" He looked at me appealingly, features keen and cold beneath his sealskin hat.

"Forget her," I said.

"I can't. I never thought this would happen to me but it has. It's . . . it's an irresistible force. In other words," he said, voice surprised at his own words, "I'm in love with her."

"Harry, you only met her yesterday."

"And she feels the same."

"How do you know?"

"I just know."

"Why are you asking my advice? You haven't the slightest intention of taking it."

"I just hoped you would advise me to do what I'm going to do anyway," he replied with a boyish grin.

I shrugged. "Well, you know how it is. If you take her out, take her back to your apartment the KGB will know immediately. Do you realise that she might suffer?"

"Not if she co-operates with them," he said sadly.

"Maybe she's got more sense than you," I said. "Maybe she won't go out with you".

"Oh but she will," he said. "Anna and I are going out to dinner tonight."

And so he launched himself into a love affair that he knew would be terminated abruptly; that might be used to blackmail him, humiliate him or banish him from the land. Equally she must have risked everything for love. And love it certainly was: inescapable as fate, electric, lyrical, a grand opera played with the black curtains of tragedy quivering in the wings.

Like a fallen priest, Harry plunged deeper into his passion than any member of the flock to whom he had preached, reneging on all his hard-bitten cynicism of old by suggesting that even the Kremlin might condone such feeling.

"You know it's just possible," he said one night to me, his only confidante. "Maybe even they understand about such things. Wouldn't it be great if I turned out to be the one guy to prove that at heart they're as sentimental as movie people on the night of the Oscars? The one guy to knock hell out of that granite-hearted image that everyone is at such pains to perpetuate?"

Just possible? Poor Harry, I thought. Poor Anna.

"You know it's got to end," I said to him in my apartment when it no longer mattered whether or not the bugs were tuned into our conversation.

"Sure it's got to end. We both know that. We live in different worlds. It just happens that there's been an eclipse; what we're doing has been blacked out for a while. But I tell you this, the black-out is my whole life."

Every day I expected to find a new face serving the amber and the beaming dolls behind the counter in the *Beryozka* shop; every day I expected to hear that Harry had been denounced for corrupting the morals of a flower of Soviet womanhood. For there was no way that the KGB could not have known about the two of them. The love affair continued for three months. Quite openly. They shared, they were an entity.

And it wasn't the reality of the inevitable ending that shocked: it was its manner: Harry was removed from Russia not by the Kremlin but by his employers in the U.S. — he was posted to Vietnam. He didn't protest because there was no point; in journalism you don't. Nor, so he told me, did Anna because, from the start, they had both been fatalistic. They had taken what had been handed to them across the counter of the *Beryozka* shop and they had spent it.

What lay ahead of them was what they had been used to before they met. At the airport they touched what they had been given for the last time; then he was gone. I met him again

129

years later in London and he told me that not once during the three months he had spent with Anna had the secret police in any way interfered.

"Like I said, they're as sentimental as movie people. Don't ever typecast people, not even the KGB!"

He put his hand in his trouser pocket and pulled out a nugget of honey-coloured amber. He felt it, put it to his cheek. "They say it keeps the warmth of the owner's body," he said.

XII

Winter was still implacably holding spring at bay in Moscow when I embarked on two big ego trips: I was asked to take part in a film and, indirectly, to become a spy.

The news that I was going to be a film star considerably enhanced my standing in the household on Kutuzovsky Prospect. *Star* was, perhaps, an exaggeration — I only had three lines, one of them little more than a grunt — but that was the status I was accorded by Dima, Valentina and Vladimir. Another *star* was Gilbert Lewthwaite. He, like me, had been asked to join the cast of the movie because the first-choice American correspondents in Moscow had all refused.

The Americans believed that immediately the film was completed their lines would be falsely dubbed. That instead of a crisp: "Give me the city desk," into a telephone they would be heard to bellow: "Death to the Capitalish warmongers in Washington." They had a point: the film was to be called *Son of a Communist*.

But neither Gilbert nor I was plagued by a suspicious nature. We saw the film as material for a feature; if they did change our lines that in itself would make a news story. Our editors agreed and we signed contracts guaranteeing us seventy roubles (about thirty pounds) a day during shooting.

The film was being made to mark the Fiftieth anniversary of the Revolution. It was therefore very prestigious although the story line was hardly stimulating. As far as we could make out it concerned a go-ahead factory manager who tried to beat the system and promptly got the sack.

Gilbert and I played the parts of American correspondents questioning this mortified innovator at a Press conference and my most telling line was: "Sir, does this mean an end to your career?"

Valentina was transported by the glamorous ambience that had suddenly descended on the apartment. She arrived early, brought me eggs and bacon in bed, watched me devour every mouthful and gave me great hugs of encouragement as I set off for the studios. No longer do I harbour much sympathy for those stars who complain about the attentions of teeny-boppers. It is one thing to have the sleeve of your jacket torn off: it is quite another to have your rib cage compressed every morning by twenty stones of Soviet womanhood. As she squeezed I felt my well-rehearsed lines expelled from my throat in a hiss of pain.

Vladimir was impressed but less demonstrably so. It was, I suppose, confusing for a KGB agent to find an Englishman playing the part of an American in a Russian film. But he accompanied me to the studio on a couple of occasions; with his sleek hair and powerful frame garbed in blue mohair he looked more like a film star than anyone else on the set.

But it was Dima who benefited most. He had to accompany me as an interpreter and he was also paid seventy roubles a day. The money was deposited in a tin box in his desk and I wondered how much longer the Abominable Snowman could hold out against such financial resources.

The film was in the hands of one of the country's leading directors, a small, balding man with an agile tongue and a repertoire of histrionic gestures. The star was a tall, grey-haired actor, sophisticated and sad-eyed, who spent most of his time off the set chatting up Diane.

Our big scene was in a bar. It was constructed of cardboard and the brandy we tossed back was cold tea. After a chaotic first day I made a stand and demanded real brandy. The director punched a cardboard wall but, after voluble protestations, finally agreed.

What blunted the fine edge of my performance was my inability to pick up my cue in Russian. Here Gilbert had the advantage because he could by now — or so he claimed — read Noddy to his children in Russian. The result was that the star would make some soulful reply to a question from another correspondent whereupon I would bound to my feet and demand, completely out of context: "Sir, does this mean an end to your career?"

For the first half dozen or so times I inserted great intensity into this question. But as it was almost always uttered at the wrong juncture I began to feel more like a heckler at Hyde Park Corner than another Olivier or Gielgud.

After three days the part really began to have a traumatic effect on me. At home Diane would ask whether I wanted steak or chicken for dinner and I would stare at her, eyes glittering, fists clenched, and intone: "Does this mean an end to your career?" And in my sleep I would mutter the question throughout the night. Finally the director, who by this time was also drinking brandy instead of cold tea, instructed an extra to tap his nose when I was expected to utter my lines.

One other stumbling-block was our accents. Mine was unmistakably London; Gilbert's was as North Country as Black Pudding. The trouble was that we had to speak with a cross-Atlantic drawl. Gilbert's *bête noire* was Arkansas.

The scene would be bubbling along while the director listened, hands clasped in prayer, until Gilbert had to make a fleeting reference to that particular state of America. Suddenly he would bellow: "Cut," rounding on Gilbert, at the same time pounding the long-suffering section of cardboard wall with his fist and enunciate in a voice that sounded close to hysteria: "Ark-an-saw, Gaspadeen Lewthwaite, not Ark-an-sas."

When our scenes were finally finished the director bade us farewell with visible relief. The movie was, I believe, a success — it *had* to be — but by the time it was shown I had left Russia.

Oddly Gilbert eventually joined the staff of an American newspaper. I'm sure he prospered because he was unquestionably one of the most able newspapermen I encountered. And I'm sure his editors were impressed by his ready pronunciation of ARK-AN-SAW.

The return to workaday reporting after these heady experiences was softened by an apparent attempt to enlist me as a spy. My spymaster was a British businessman, bulky and intimidating, with a taste for chalk-stripe suits. He came to the apartment for lunchtime drinks and suggested that we might take a walk — the accepted ploy to escape surveillance.

The earmuffs of his fur hat didn't really harmonise with his black Crombie and, strolling along Kutuzovsky Prospect, stabbing at stray scraps of paper with his umbrella like a park attendant, he lost much of his presence.

"Like it here?" he asked.

"Marvellous." A reaction which never failed to astonish Westerners.

"Good", he said, spearing a paper bag with his umbrella. "That's what we like to hear."

"That's what who likes to hear?"

"But do you approve of everything here? You know, the system and all that."

"Of course not," I said.

"Good," he said.

"But there's a lot I do approve of."

"Ah-hah." He removed the paper bag from the umbrella and we watched it flutter across the street. "You haven't any

134

inclinations that way, I suppose?"

"What way?"

"Their way."

"Good God no."

"Good," he said.

"That's what you like to hear?"

"I believe you're due for some leave," he said.

"How did you know that?"

He smiled mysteriously. "Maybe we could meet when you come over. Have a drink or two at my club."

"That would be nice," I said.

"Get to meet people do you?"

"I am a reporter."

"Influential people?"

"I haven't met Brezhnev˜ yet."

(I had tried but my requests for an interview had been ignored.)

"But you get around."

"Oh yes," I said airily, "I get around all right."

"Interesting," he said, unsuccessfully trying to impale a cigarette packet. "Here take this." He plunged his hand inside his overcoat and handed me a visiting card. "Give me a ring when you get back."

"For any particular reason?" I asked.

"Bloody cold, isn't it," he said turning and heading back towards the apartment.

For the next couple of weeks, feeling like Wormwold in Graham Greene's *Our Man in Havana*, I debated this sinister exchange. There didn't seem to be much doubt that he wanted to recruit me into Western Intelligence; but I couldn't understand why because I didn't have access to anything more clandestine than Valentina's grocery bill. But perhaps he had in mind *drops* in the countryside; micro-dots in my correspondence . . .

135

Not that there was anything particularly secret about the identities of the espionage agents in Moscow: everyone understood that all military attachés were spies: why else were they there? Probably the only difference in the Soviet espionage organisation in London and the Western set-up in Moscow was that whereas all the Russian diplomats were spies only about a quarter of ours were engaged in espionage.

When Diane and I went back to England on a fortnight's leave I told a taxi driver at London Airport to take us to a good pub for the night. I imagined oak timbers, mullioned windows and pints of nutty draught beer beneath clerical collars of foam.

Instead the driver took us to an odd establishment on Tagg's Island on the Thames. It was a dilapidated hotel with a mysterious reception staff who muttered into the telephone: "Can't speak now," and hung up whenever we approached. Assuming that the cab driver was employed by MI6, I telephoned the businessman who had given me his card.

"We've been expecting you," he said. "Where are you?"

"Don't you know?"

"I wouldn't ask if I knew," he said tetchily.

"On Tagg's Island," I told him.

"Good God, what are you doing there?"

We arranged to meet in two days time, not at his club but at Hampton Court which was presumably unbugged.

While we waited for the rendezvous Diane and I enjoyed England. The freedom. The sense of the ridiculous. The extrovert pub debates. The green, rain-soaked smells beside the river. We even solved the mystery lurking behind the reception desk: the staff were placing bets.

Finally I met my contact near the maze. He was hatless but, apart from that, dressed as he was in Moscow.

"Well?" he said after a while.

"I've been thinking about it."

136

"Marvellous," he said, lunging at a stray bus ticket with his umbrella.

"It's an interesting proposition."

"Mmmmm."

"But I don't think I'm your man."

"Ah." He absorbed this. "Then in that case you won't mind me asking why you bothered to come."

"To see if you really meant it."

"Meant what?"

"You know," I said.

"Do I?" He turned and walked away towards the mist rising from the river.

XIII

We spent ten days in England. I visited my mother in Torquay, my children, my ebullient boss, David English, and the then editor of the *Express*, Derek Marks, brilliant and shy, who reprimanded me gently for not writing enough features.

I left Fleet Street at the rush hour, caught up in the crowds swarming towards their trains. I imagined the homeward-bound throngs in Moscow scrummaging with the cold and I wondered if one set of workers was really any better off than the other.

We flew back to Russia via Stockholm spending a couple of days with Lars Bringart and his wife who had returned permanently to Sweden. When we got back to Moscow there waiting for us was Lars' successor, likeable but not so cuddly, and Peter Worthington's replacement, as brash as Peter had been quiet. To these two I was the old hand; the pioneer in the wilderness, the contact with the numbers.

But soon after my return I had to leave them to fly south to the city of Alma-Ata on the Soviet border north of Kashmir and Afghanistan. And once again the invitation was indirectly at the behest of the Chinese whose relations with the Soviet Union were steadily deteriorating.

Alma-Ata is the capital of the Soviet Republic of Kazakhstan. On the other side of the Tien Shan mountains lies the province of Sinkiang, a vast province belonging to Red

138

China. According to reports from Peking there had been an Army revolt in Sinkiang against Mao Tse-tung. Thousands of refugees were said to be fleeing into Kazakhstan and it was my job to find them. The *Telegraph* had the same idea and dispatched John Miller to Alma-Ata. I took Diane and Dima.

The refugees were a people named the Uighur. But to distinguish a Uighur from a Mongolian, a Chinese, Kazakh or Tartar wasn't easy. Obviously the Russians wanted us to interview them but even Dima made little impression on such people who gazed at him curiously from placid brown eyes. They might have just escaped from the Chinese guns: on the other hand they might have been born in Alma-Ata.

We didn't have time to see much of the city. The snow was thawing prematurely and slush was knee-deep in the gutters. Near our hotel, steely bright and square, was a park, patched with snow and starved yellow grass, containing a wooden church that looked as though it had been hand carved. Around the city, like a crumpled white muff, stood the Tien Shan mountains. As dusk thickened they moved nearer.

We managed to find a refugee author named Zia Samedi who told us that the Red Guards were trying to suppress minority groups and make Sinkiang wholly Chinese. I also interviewed Ivan Spivahnov, deputy editor of the local *Pravda*, who had the gall to dismiss Chinese propaganda as "crude and clumsy."

Mindful of Derek Marks' request for more features I wrote a featurish piece, picked up the telephone in my hotel room and once again got straight through to London.

"Kazakhstan? What's the weather like out there, old man?" asked the copy-taker.

Next morning the story was projected as the lead news story on the front page. Encouraging but a debatable commentary on my feature writing abilities.

We found more refugees produced with a magician's flourish by the Russians in the market-place. Said one: "You know, we hear about the plight of some country in Africa with a few hundred thousand inhabitants and yet here we are, a nation of six million, and no one seems to care."

I took his point. A train crash in Bombay with one hundred dead is a couple of paragraphs: an underground accident at Morden with six injured is a page-lead. After the interview we wandered round the market. Alma-Ata is renowned for its apples and there they were, batteries of them, polished and red, spitting juice when you bit them. There too, in front of the vendors who lurked, lizard-faced and unblinking, in the shadows, were herbs, nuts, tough-looking cheeses, sandals with soles made from rubber tyres, shawls, boots and miracle cures. I picked up a bottle of brown fluid and asked Dima what it was for.

"For belching," he said. "To stop it, that is," he added.

It snowed heavily overnight and at dawn when we set out by taxi for the airport the snow had fused the city to the mountains. It was deep and soft and undisturbed; the rooftops were heavy with it and it had smoothed all the city's rough edges, covered its dirt, made a virgin of it once more.

The taxi pushed its way slowly to the airport like a snow-plough. A runway had already been cleared; it looked like a black canal.

We adjourned to the lounge to join the usual lethargic throng of women in headscarves and scruffy soldiers and settled down to play poker. After an hour or so it began to snow again. The snow poured from the sky blocking out the windows and jamming the doors.

Said Diane, who had been an air hostess and knew about these things: "One thing's for sure, we won't take off today."

Fifteen minutes later, with the blizzard howling around us, we were airborne.

Back in Moscow spring was poised to vanquish winter; it was almost Easter and time to try and impale the elusive spirit of religion in the Soviet Union. At Christmas it had been inviolate in its chrysalis, buried in winter; but now surely it was ready to emerge and test its wings. Snow still lay on the ground but it had a sheen to it where it had melted briefly before the icy rebuke of dusk; the skies were softer; birds were on the wing and so was hope.

The annual Easter newspaper story was hooliganism outside Russian Orthodox churches as believers attended midnight mass on the Saturday. Young louts, apparently, jeered, jostled and sometimes roughed-up the worshippers. To me this had the ring of stage-management, of rent-a-crowd hooligans. I couldn't bring myself to believe that a people so obsessed by the mystical, so superstitious, so enchanted by the ecclesiastical splendours of the past — the rich collected icons as avidly as Americans collect guns — could behave so grossly.

Indeed I had the impression that, clandestinely, a renaissance of religious fervour was under way; a movement begun, ironically, by the death of the greatest tyrant of them all, Joseph Stalin, who channelled all worship towards himself and exterminated any dissenters. But when Nikita Khrushchev subsequently tarnished Stalin's image, his bewildered adherents had their ideology knocked from under their feet and many of them returned gratefully to the altars of Christianity. Since then the relationship between State and Church had been an impassioned one, its moods ranging between paternal tolerance and repression.

It is the repression that one hears about in the West and it is therefore worth noting that there are said to be more members of the Church (about thirty million) than there are of the Communist Party in Russia. Although in the same breath it must be remembered that the Church preaches obedience to

141

the State and exists only with its sanction.

But it wasn't the parties to this compromise that I sought this Easter: I wanted to find the crusaders who knelt before the Cross and banished the Hammer and Sickle from the House of God: I wanted to see the young and inquisitive who, while remaining steadfastly patriotic, didn't accept that religion and politics were inseparable. And the way to achieve this was emphatically not to attend a church service endangered by thugs and staged by Party stalwarts to remind religious leaders not to exceed their brief.

Word reached me from various 'usually reliable sources' about the location this year of a mass that was sure to be well attended. By worshippers and hoodlums, I supposed. Dima inquired with studied nonchalance whether I would be attending and I told him I hadn't yet made up my mind. I decided that secretly he hoped I wouldn't because he didn't want to witness his compatriots intimidating an innocent congregation. And intimidate them they undoubtedly would because the official Party press was currently mounting a campaign against such religious excesses as baptisms. Not to mention church weddings and funerals which were gaining favour. Vladimir and Victor Louis also inquired by telephone but again I was vague, implying that as the harrassment occurred every year it was hardly news.

On the evening of Easter Saturday Diane and I drove beneath cold stars to a church on the outskirts of the city in the opposite direction to the one used as a stage prop by the Soviet publicists. It wasn't architecturally noble but it was cosy with a dome that, in the moonlight, looked like a bubble that had just landed there and an interior that glowed with candlelight like a Halloween pumpkin.

What *was* notable was the stream of worshippers — and spectators — pouring into the church. Not just the old whom one expected to see because they were exempt from victimisa-

142

tion but the young and the middle-aged. And in the aureole of the candlelight, beneath the moon and the stars, their faces lost their wariness, their clothes their shabbiness, they were about to celebrate the Resurrection and not even the manifest presence of uniformed militia, or the intangible presence of the KGB (for undoubtedly they were among us) could break the spell. Come to that, even the militia looked benign.

We joined the throng and Diane began to talk to a young girl with questing blue eyes and thick blonde hair curling from beneath a fur hat, trying to find out whether it was curiosity or devotion that had brought her to the church. She replied in thickly-accented English. Curiosity, she said, had been her original motive; but now she felt the stirring of ancient beliefs.

"As though fog had suddenly cleared from in front of a cathedral," she said.

"Do you think this feeling will stay with you?" I asked her.

"Perhaps. I shall have to wait and see. But I don't see why not because it is part of our heritage." Her words caught fire. "Religion is our roots, politics the flower that withers," or words to that effect.

I looked around anxiously because I didn't want to be responsible for getting her into trouble with the secret police; but the crowd around us continued to push sturdily forward, apparently not understanding her words.

"Aren't you afraid of being seen here?"

"Why should I be?" she demanded with spirit. "Religion is not banned in the Soviet Union; in fact it is encouraged."

"But surely it is a pale shadow of what religion should be. You know, when you go to church you shouldn't have to worship God *and* the State."

"Poof. Who does? The Church may have come to terms with the Party — lip-service, I believe you call it — but you surely don't imagine that when people kneel in front of the altar they are paying homage to Communism?"

143

I didn't think so because to worship God and Karl Marx was surely a contradiction in terms. Nor did I think the girl was speaking from experience because religious fervour had only just stirred in her breast. But I did think she was speaking from second-hand knowledge, and that in itself was encouraging.

Inside the church the congregation, all standing, were packed as close as the rush-hour crowd on the London underground. We breathed incense and burning tallow and white-washed mustiness; we heard an invisible choir; we gazed humbly at red and gold icons; we bowed our heads, mesmerised by the chanting of the two priests, black beards as thick as mufflers above their spun-gold vestments. Through the portals of the church we had entered the past, deep and dark and perfumed; we were in the indestructible vaults of Russia and all that lay above was but leaves in the wind. And in these undisturbed regions our senses melted until we felt only the pulse of Mother Russia.

The mass lasted several hours and, although deeply moved, I was guiltily relieved that we had not arrived at the beginning. At the end of the service the priests emerged into the frosty night and led the congregation, bearing candles, three times round the church; an enactment, I was told, of the search for the body of Christ in the Holy Sepulchre. We drove home in silence, still deep in a holy trance.

None of my Russian contacts inquired the following day whether I had witnessed the harassment of the faithful at the appointed church. They knew, of course, that I had witnessed a far more important phenomenon: a symbolic resurrection that might one day lose its symbolism and spread across the land.

*   *   *

Towards the end of April winter finally capitulated. And

144

Moscow became a water carnival. Water surged along the gutters, raced down the drain-pipes; parks became lakes, the side streets rivers. And everywhere the water played its music and laughed at itself. The river was crowded with jostling ice-floes; great envelopes of snow fell from the roofs to splash ponderously in newly-spawned ponds.

In the evenings the city froze again and at dawn the puddles were tissued with ice and windows were fringed with thin icicles that began to drip with the first touch of sun. But this was rearguard action: spring was here with summer at its heels.

Frenziedly the Muscovites embraced the two because, as always, their joint visit would be short. Off went the fur hats, the heavy coats and felt boots. And for two weeks they joyously padded through the waters of Moscow in goloshes as shiny wet as seals' paws.

As soon as the water had receded flowers bloomed, grass sprang alive and the river, having shed its ice, stepped out as carelessly as a pretty girl in a park. The golden cupolas of the Kremlin gathered up the sunshine, refurbished it, regenerated it. Armadas of white clouds assembled on the borders of the bright blue sky but never invaded; green leaves appeared among the matchstick stems of the silver birch and spun secret glades.

In Gorky Park the ferris wheel took shrieking girls and protective young men up to the sky and back; pleasure boats butted their way through the mossy waters of the lake; soldiers and sailors with the faces of thirteen republics marched, brave and bareheaded, along the pathways while strolling players strummed their guitars and the old men, brooding over their chessboards, broke their torpor with sudden, venomous strikes.

As the heat settled over the city like a warm wet cloth its people took to the beaches of the Moscow River. Beaches

145

which were flat and clean, holding back forests of pine and birch from the deep, fat curves of the river.

Throughout this respite from winter these beaches were as busy as Brighton on a Bank Holiday Monday. Beer and fizzy drinks frothed from the cafés, vendors of ice-creams and *kvas* took up positions reserved from last year and the fresh, mud-smelling air vibrated with the impact of table-tennis balls on the green tables at the rear of the beaches.

Sunbathing wasn't a passion: it was an obsession. Not only did the snow-pale Muscovites lie like contortionists to allow the sun access to every decent part of their bodies, they leaned, arms outstretched, against walls, crucified there to grill the insides of biceps and forearms. Women freed from the tyranny of corsets expanded joyously in brassieres and knickers; young girls paraded shyly in new bikinis. But they all treated the sun with respect: they made nosecaps and hats from copies of *Pravda* and they retreated into the resinous depths of the forest when the heat became too fierce. There at dusk, perhaps, they bowed low to the setting sun which they worshipped more fervently than any gods of religion or ideology.

We journalists were allowed to use the nearby diplomatic beach where foreigners could follow their decadent pursuits without corrupting Soviet citizens. Thus the ghettos moved to the riverside, reporters, diplomats, businessmen and tame spies, as effectively isolated as they were in the city.

Diane and I, however, often crossed these sandy frontiers illegally to join the Russians who seemed to be enjoying themselves more than the foreigners in their rarefied precinct. We played table-tennis, guzzled and gorged, swam in deep green water and, taking the sun, watched the big white pleasure boats — floating havens, we were told, for sexual promiscuity — sailing grandly past, surely on their way to the Mississipi.

Lack of privacy was the only drawback to a day on the

146

Russian beaches. Retiring on one occasion to a ramshackle lavatory made of corrugated iron I found that the facilities consisted of a plank with twelve holes cut in it placed over a drain.

Eleven of the holes were occupied by Russian men going about their business, trousers round their ankles, newspapers in their hands. In a bizarre sort of way they looked like businessmen on the 8 a.m. to Waterloo minus their pants.

Deciding to forego the pleasure of occupying the twelfth hole I stumbled out into the sunshine, *Daily Express* beneath my arm. Outside a stocky man with a sun-reddened face grabbed me by the shoulder and said: "As is well known you shouldn't be here."

"At the moment," I said, "I don't want to be." I summoned Diane and returned to the diplomatic beach where at least there was a modicum of protocol attached to such functions.

*   *   *

The main event heralding summer was the May Day parade in Red Square. Except for the weather it was much the same as the November parade to mark the anniversary of the Revolution. What struck me was the comparison between the military might unfurled across the Square and the frailty of the intellects assembled there.

Predictably the Defence Minister, Marshal Malinovsky, attacked the Chinese. Predictably Chinese diplomats stood up and walked out. Hardly an edifying lesson in power politics. Just like the November parade, the May Day display was like an overlong banquet: the first course — giant rockets, tanks and massed ranks of immaculately drilled soldiers — was awesome, rousing: the dessert gave you indigestion.

But despite this gluttony of achievement the May Day parade, with its seasonal dressing of hope, does illustrate the motivation of the Russian people.

The obvious question that surfaces after a few weeks in Russia is: why in God's name do the people put up with the deal they get from Communism? The shoddy goods, the surveillance, the curtailment of liberty . . .

The answer has nothing to do with the dull creed that rules them. It is simply Patriotism. With the red banners snapping in the breeze, military bands playing and marching feet stamping out their parade ground rhythms this national pride leaps to attention as proud as an anthem.

The Russians are, perhaps, the most patriotic nation in the world. Stoically, as they have done for centuries, they endure yet another tyranny wearing another garb. And when they pay homage to Marx or Lenin they are secretly paying their respects to the tortured soul of Russia. How can they think otherwise when one day Stalin is a saviour, the next a despot?

Alongside this pride stands its partner, shame. And it is shame that also accounts for the apparent docility of the Russian temperament that confounds the West. Acutely aware of our superior living standards, they seem willing to put up with any domestic deprivations to enable their country to gain ascendancy in the arms race and in space.

What's more, these flames of patriotism are kindled from the cradle. In the kindergartens — a proper schooling doesn't begin until children are seven — three-year-olds will be introduced to Uncle Lenin. And what better figurehead than this omnipresent deity who was fierce, avuncular, noble and prophetic. In the last war we needed a Churchill: the Russians still need one and with the memory of Lenin they possess a comparable inspiration.

The nursery school awakening of patriotism takes a dramatic political turn when at the age of nine the children are enlisted into the Young Pioneers: boy scouts with a cause. In the May Day parade I watched them swarming across Red

148

Square towards the spun-sugar baubles of St. Basil's, red scarves fluttering above their white shirts.

At first it seemed infinitely sad to me that these children were marching to the drum beats of an ideology imposed arbitrarily upon them; that in their teens many of them would march unquestioningly into the Komsomol, the Young Communist League, and thence into an existence where it is a crime to question.

But that was before the spirit of this swaggering day infected me and I realised that, whether they appreciated it or not, they were responding to a call more ancient and emotive than any political summons.

And that is what the West has to realise: it is not necessarily pitted against a creed, it is matched against chauvinism written in blood.

*   *   *

The Red Square rallies were always a testing time for western military experts and the foreign journalists and diplomats.

On the eve of the parades the vast Soviet weaponry was parked, hooded and menacing, around Red Square. Clutching identification documents as though they might deflect bullets, the experts prowled the night streets seeking clues to any new devices for obliterating New York or London.

Later the journalists filed stories to their offices while the military attachés dispatched coded messages to their governments. Such assessments were perplexing to correspondents such as myself who barely understood the mechanics of a flintstone musket let alone a nuclear missile.

Anticipating penetrating questions from the foreign desk I telephoned Vladimir and asked him if there was going to be any new hardware on show.

"*Niet,*" he said firmly.

"Sure?"

"Have I ever misled you?"

Not as far as I knew he hadn't.

When the anticipated call came from London and I was asked about the latest instrument of annihilation I said with magnificent assurance: "There won't be anything new."

A pause. They were not accustomed to such authoritative statements from me.

"Are you sure, old man?"

"Perfectly."

"But the agencies are saying —"

"There will be nothing new," I repeated.

"Can you give us a paragraph to that effect?"

"Of course," and I dictated the paragraph, defying all the experts and writing my notice of recall if I were wrong.

The following day confirmation came from Washington, Whitehall and Bonn that the considered verdict was that nothing new had been displayed on Red Square.

I gazed across the sun warmed rooftops of Moscow and smiled. Summer had come.

XIV

As the windows were unsealed and opened wide, the vases filled with flowers, an atmosphere of taut anticipation settled on the household.

Not only was the foreign editor, David English, coming to visit us but the British Ambassador, Sir Geoffrey Harrison, had indicated that he would attend a buffet supper I was throwing. Valentina turned the colour of a Victoria plum and moaned softly to herself whenever she remembered the honours bestowed upon us; Diane retreated behind a shelf of cookery books; Dima rehearsed stiff little speeches better suited for the Court of St James's.

The reason for all this belated recognition was an exchange of photographers between the *Daily Express* and the Soviet agency *Novosti*. Bill Lovelace of the *Express* was to work with *Novosti* in Moscow; *Novosti*'s Lev Nosov was to fly to London.

The person least affected by the preparations, as nerve-racking as rehearsals for a first night, was myself because I was plucked from the traumas by a series of news stories.

The most important of these concerned the forty year-old Soviet cosmonaut, Vladimir Komarov, whose spaceship Soyuz 1 was expected to link up with another man-made satellite. By midday on the day of the appointment in space newsmen began to suspect that all was not well because news of the link-up was long overdue. When *Izvestia* failed to appear on the streets by 4 p.m., its normal publication time, we smelled disaster. At 5 p.m. it was announced that *Izvestia* would not be published at all.

Agencies began to put out speculative stories; my office asked me to elucidate. All I could suggest was that Komarov, who three years earlier had experienced an irregular heart-beat, might have suffered a coronary. At 5.23 Tass broke the story: "Cosmonaut Vladimir Komarov has perished when completing the test flight of the spaceship Soyuz." At 5.24 they repeated the flash.

But Komarov, a stocky unpretentious family man, hadn't died from a heart attack. According to a later communiqué the parachute ropes on the spacecraft had become tangled 23,000 feet above the earth.

The story, shared with Ross Mark in Washington and Antony Buzek in London, made the splash with another piece from Moscow across an inside page. This was followed by the tribute paid by tens of thousands of Muscovites to Komarov's ashes in a silver casket in the Red Army Hall and the funeral when those ashes were placed in the walls of the Kremlin.

Meanwhile preparations for the celebrations at Kutuzovsky Prospect 15 proceeded tortuously and it was difficult to determine whose reputation made mistress and staff the more apprehensive: foreign editor or British Ambassador.

The Ambassador just had the edge, I decided, because although it wasn't the first visit by a foreign editor to the apartment, Sir Geoffrey Harrison had never before attended a journalist's party.

Shortly before David English was due to arrive I was introduced to Lev Nosov, lean, crew-cut and correct, with instructions to prepare him for the hurly-burly of British journalism. He listened unbelievingly to my tales illustrating the competitive spirit of Fleet Street and responded by creating a fiasco at Sheremetyevo airport. He claimed to know the airport as no other; when we drove there to meet English he knew just where we should station ourselves to be able to greet him immediately he had completed embarkation formalities.

All over the world English had been greeted by smoothly efficient correspondents who had ushered him to a waiting limousine, driven him to a plush hotel and taken him on perfectly timed conducted tours of their outposts. Such treatment was his due and he expected it.

Mindful of this, I began to shuffle uneasily when, half an hour after the plane from London landed, there was still no sign of him.

"Are you sure this is where we should wait?" I asked Nosov.

"It is well known," he said.

As he spoke English materialised behind me carrying his bags and said: "Where in the hell have you been?"

I looked to Nosov for an explanation but he merely shook his head sadly.

English looked as jaunty as ever but beneath his extrovert manner I could detect reproof. Particularly when he told me that he had been greeted by almost every British journalist in Moscow — out at the airport to interview another visiting VIP — except his own representative.

Making light of it, I introduced him to Nosov and said: "Old Lev here will explain." Old Lev did no such thing and broodingly we made our way to the car.

In Paris, Washington or Rome, English would have been whisked to his hotel in some gleaming sedan. Which explained the ruminative expression on his features when he beheld the grey Cortina, one wing still buckled from its encounter with the taxi. The damaged door opened with a noise like an inn sign creaking in the wind and English climbed in.

I was by this time on the brink of a breakdown. "First time

in Moscow?" I asked brightly as the starting motor groaned dismally.

"First time," he said, adding: "Your battery's flat."

I made clicking noises with my tongue. "It's been a terrible winter."

"What's that got to do with it?"

"Nothing really," I said as the engine miraculously fired.

Revving wildly I gave English a fierce smile, engaged the gears — and backed into the car parked behind me.

The following day I escaped to the Tartar capital of Kazan. I had previously applied for permission to visit one of the small communities of Britons working in the Soviet Union. Happily permission was granted as preparations for the buffet supper were reaching a crescendo.

I apologised to English for departing at such a crucial time, pointing out that I owed it to the *Express* to make the trip. English regarded me cynically but agreed, probably because he didn't relish another course in stock-car racing in the streets of Moscow.

Kazan was a dusty, disappointing city and the Britons who lived in small, hot apartments were understandably depressed by their circumstances. There were twenty-one of them supervising the construction of a plastics plant and they described themselves as the Legion of the Lost. "As far as the British Embassy is concerned," one of them told me, "we don't exist."

They had asked for beer, books and magazines but none had arrived. I wrote the story and telephoned it to London with instructions that it shouldn't be printed until after the British Ambassador had attended my supper.

When I arrived at Kazan airport on the day of the supper to fly back to Moscow I was told that my flight was indefinitely postponed. I telephoned Diane to tell her that I might not be able to make it and then called Vladimir. A few hours later the flight was called. It may well have been that the aircraft had been repaired; on the other hand it might have been due to KGB influence.

I landed in Moscow one and a half hours before the guests were due and drove the Cortina at suicidal speed to Kutuzovsky Prospect.

In my absence miracles had been performed. The buffet was a banquet; snacks of black and red caviar, smoked salmon and tongue waited in the wings; the Chi Chi bar was an alcoholic's paradise. Hothouse flowers bloomed in the vases, soft music issued from the antique record-player, dirt and dust had been banished to Siberia.

But the spectacle wasn't quite flawless: there under the television was the sugar-coated redcurrant. And I was glad to see it; it had by now acquired a mystique — I felt that if ever it disappeared from the apartment then I would vanish from Moscow.

Valentina and another plump maid from the UPKD, both dressed in black and white like old-time Lyons' nippies, hovered anxiously in the background; Dima and Vladimir, freshly combed, pressed and shaved, stood guard at the entrance to the cavernous lounge. Diane in a costume tailored from green raw silk she had bought in Bombay wandered around touching things. It was like a stage set before the curtain rises. Five minutes later it was like the celebration party after a smash-hit.

Guests poured into the apartment. British diplomats, journalists and businessmen and, miraculously, Russians by the coachload. For a few seconds old adversaries eyed each other guardedly over their drinks; then the vodka and champagne exploded into exuberant geniality. If the leaders of Communism and Capitalism could have been transported into the apartment that evening they would have signed options on peace for the next thousand years.

Sir Geoffrey Harrison, a classic ambassador, silver-haired, wily and suave, met Russians in the most uninhibited atmosphere he had encountered in Moscow; Lev Nosov met his counterpart from London, Bill Lovelace, a benign, chunky photographer who was later to win the Photographer of the Year award in Britain; David English beamed upon the scene, the entrepreneur reviewing his spectacular.

The buffet that had taken days to prepare vanished as swiftly as a child's hoard of sweets at the end of Lent and, after Sir Geoffrey had departed, reserved Britons and stolid Russians danced, sang, embraced, wept and made a mockery of two decades of international enmity.

When they had all gone Valentina, Dima, Vladimir, Diane and I grinned at each other, as smug as well-fed monks. I proposed a toast to us and did what I had always wanted to do: I hurled my empty glass against the wall.

Next day Diane and I took English to the Bolshoi Ballet. We hadn't allowed ourselves too much time and, as I drove across the city, I remembered that if you were late the doors were shut with rude finality in your face.

Ten minutes before the curtain was due to rise a policeman waved me down near Red Square and pointed with his truncheon at the wrecked and rusting wing of the Cortina.

I wound down the window and he peered in, talking rapidly and angrily, punctuating his diatribe with petulant blows with his truncheon on the twisted metal.

While English stared aloofly ahead scarcely acknowledging the presence of the disgruntled militiaman I turned to Diane and asked her what he was saying.

"He says it's an offence to drive a damaged car," she said.

"What does he want me to do?"

"Mend it," she said.

"Now?"

English intervened. "Diane," he said with glacial authority, "you do not speak Russian. Nor does Derek, nor do I."

The policeman was becoming increasingly excited. We all shook our heads at him and spread wide our hands. He gave the wing another couple of cracks, produced a notebook the way movie detectives used to and made a note of the registration number of the car that clearly indicated that I was a foreign journalist.

Then he waved us on with a gesture implying that we should prepare an overnight bag for a stay in the white-tiled cells of Lubyanka Prison. By now we had four minutes in which to take our seats at the Bolshoi. Once again I manoeuvred the car like a stunt driver while English, arms folded, maintained his icy composure.

I parked the car in a non-parking area, pulled Diane out of the rear seat and pushed English towards the colonnades of the theatre breezily muttering gibberish into his ear. Perhaps he wasn't aware of the severity of the punishment for being late; perhaps he merely wanted to test the mettle of one of his men in a crisis; whatever the reason he didn't respond to the emergency and I felt that at any moment he might stop and deliver Hamlet's soliloquy.

Pushing English and pulling Diane, I hurled myself into the theatre, ducked under the arm of an usherette and charged the stairs. We took our seats in our box as the curtain rose.

"Well," I said idiotically, "we just caught the edition."

"Which is all that matters," English said as the orchestra beneath us sounded my reprieve.

XV

Bill Lovelace brought with him to Moscow competitive journalism of a ferocity not normally encountered outside London, Manchester and Glasgow.

The *Daily Mirror* had decided not to allow the *Express* exclusive photographic rights to Russia through its deal with *Novosti* and had dispatched to Moscow a picture-hungry Cockney cameraman named Kent Gavin, also a Photographer of the Year.

The Russians helped both Lovelace and Gavin and sat back to enjoy the fight. And instead of the leisurely pursuit of feature pictures to mark the fiftieth anniversary of the Revolution Lovelace's assignment developed into a frenetic hard-news-style scramble with me labouring in his wake.

Every day Lovelace, placid exterior masking nimble journalistic instincts, would rush film to Sheremetyevo airport to be air-freighted to London; every day he would meet Gavin, wolfishly astute, doing the same.

Only in the evening did Lovelace relax. He had brought with him a dart-board and a couple of sets of darts. Vladimir who claimed he had never played before immediately challenged Lovelace to a match with fifty roubles at stake. Lovelace, who had been spearing treble-twenties in pubs since he left kindergarten, accepted the challenge with unseemly haste, but he failed to get a double with his first three darts.

Vladimir the hunter stripped off his mohair jacket, smoothed the wings of his sleek black hair and faced the board. He drew one hand behind his head like a javelin-thrower apparently intent on throwing the dart through the wall and into the kitchen. But he didn't see a board there: he saw the golden eye of a tiger, the heart-beat of a moose.

His first dart thudded into the double-twenty. The dart-board shuddered. Vladimir controlled his breathing, regained his balance — and flung his second arrow into the treble-twenty. And the third. Lovelace paid up gamely but thereafter devoted himself to the daily war of attrition with the *Mirror*. Half way through this the two of us were ordered to fly to Georgia.

The *Express* had heard that Russian athletes were training for the 1968 Olympics in the Caucasus Mountains in Georgia to acclimatize themselves illegally to the conditions they would experience in Mexico. To travel to Georgia we had to obtain permits, and give *bona fide* reasons for our visit: to invent a plausible excuse for flying one thousand one hundred miles to Tbilisi and driving thousands of feet up in the mountains required ingenuity.

The fact that the Russians viewed our intention of 'getting local colour' with scepticism was emphasised by our Intourist guide in Tbilisi who, as we were hiring a car, said: "You know you're wasting your time, don't you. There aren't any athletes up there," gesturing towards the mountains. "Why don't you stay in Tbilisi and have a good time?"

It was a tempting offer. Tbilisi is a fascinating city breathing with rebellion and intrigue — but to any self-respecting journalist a denial, especially an unsolicited one, is a challenge that cannot be ignored. So off we set, feeling lost without Dima and guilty because this was Yeti country; but we hadn't brought him because we couldn't make him party to a conspiracy.

159

The driver took us at a steady pace through the wild green mountains. We climbed higher and higher, while the suspicion that the mission was doomed stiffened. Four hours later we stopped on a grassy plateau which should have been alive with Herculean endeavour. But the only occupant was a small, brown-skinned man with a postage-stamp moustache who looked barely capable of climbing out of bed.

He greeted the driver and guide perfunctorily as though they regularly brought lunatics to this desolate spot to observe invisible athletes and beckoned us with an emaciated hand to follow him. In a hut a dozen stalwart Georgians and one pretty girl with curly hair and flirtatious eyes were waiting for us. Soon the sport that *was* practised here among the razored peaks became apparent: drinking.

Compared to Georgian tipplers Muscovites are 'wine-tasters'. But the Georgians are true southerners, equipped with swaggering and elegant decadence to which the Kremlin turns a hooded eye. They look like bandits — Stalin was a Georgian — they intrigue with tortuous application, they dress raffishly and they are the unchallenged masters of *blat*.

Moustaches bristling, eyes knowing in their brigands' faces, the men lined up to begin a succession of toasts with tumblerfuls of Kinzmarauli wine, the red and lethal elixir of Georgia. This was to be our punishment for our assumptions.

I never knew the identities of our welcoming committee but, as the wine slid down my throat, it mattered less and less. In between each toast we ate kebab, roasted chicken legs and slices of pork and talked. They spoke English and I even found a few Russian phrases floating on the tide of red wine.

Slyly I took the girl aside and asked her what she had done with all the athletes. She laughed. "Poof," she said, "we make them disappear like that," snapping her fingers.

More toasts. Hazily I realised that our hosts were conserving their strength: whereas we drank every time — and the tumbler had to be drained — only a few of them at a time raised their glasses. We drank to Stalin, disgraced everywhere in the Soviet Union except Georgia; to the Queen and her husband and family; to Anglo-Soviet friendship; to the *Daily Express*; to George Orwell, Karl Marx, John Wayne and Paddington Bear.

In between toasts I slipped in questions about Olympic training which were countered by gusts of laughter. The last toast that I could recall was to: 'The Phantom Runners'. By then the Georgian revenge for our duplicity was almost complete. We were loaded semi-conscious into the car and driven down the mountain road.

Half way to Tbilisi I surfaced groggily and told the driver to stop so that I could relieve myself. Bill Lovelace slept on with a beautiful smile on his face.

On the roadside I made my way towards a tree, missed it — and fell down a mountain.

Cartwheeling, somersaulting, sliding, I careered down a near-precipice until I hit another tree far below my original target. There I did what I had to do and turned to begin my ascent. But the mountainside was a wall. I took one step up and two back. I sat down philosophically. I had enjoyed a good life; here I would perish, perhaps glimpsing in my last conscious moments the Abominable Snowman lurching towards me through the pine trees.

Above I vaguely heard shouts. I glanced up and saw a human chain reaching towards me. A rope came snaking down. "Tie it round your waist," the driver shouted. I did so, And up I went like a frog out of a pump.

The driver had enlisted the help of some peasants who regarded me with awe as I dramatically materialised on the road beside them. I was probably the first western imperialist they had seen and if I was typical, their expressions said, then *Pravda* had understated the case about our decadence. I waved to them and, like Royalty, settled in the back of the car beside the recumbent form of Bill Lovelace. But the revenge was not quite over.

For two hours we slept in our neat, cheerful hotel. Then we were awoken by a fresh shift of Georgian hosts and escorted round the cobbled streets, alleys and squares of the city which, with their wrought-iron balconies and dark beckoning shops, were still untouched by the dead hands of the Soviet architects.

We were taken up Mount Mtatsminda by funicular to gaze down at the green waters of the Kura river that divides the city. Then we were taken to a banquet!

In the centre of a round table in a restaurant as elegantly ornate as the Café Royal stood a great bowl of punch in which apples and grapes bobbed like corks.

"A toast," said the new, fierce-eyed host, "to the glorious independence of Georgia."

We could, of course, have refused. If we had our disembowelled bodies would probably have been found in the gutter. "To Georgia," we cried, tossing back tumblerfuls of punch. Somewhere inside me Blackpool Illuminations were switched on.

Our plates were now piled high with glistening black mounds of caviar and slices of smoked trout. But at last our stomachs rebelled. We fled to our room, locked the door, and died for the rest of the night. When we appeared like corpses in the restaurant next morning we ordered coffee.

But that old Georgian hospitality wasn't going to let us get away with that. "What you need," said the Intourist guide, "is a typical Georgian breakfast." And with a flourish the waiter set before each of us a raw onion, a chunk of cheese and a carafe of brandy.

The Russians may or may not have been training at that lonely platform in the skies. But if ever eating and drinking is introduced competitively into the Olympic Games no one else

162

need bother to train: the gold medal belongs to Georgia.

*   *   *

On my return to Moscow I started clandestine work again on the novel which I had entrusted to Diane during my absence. It was to be about the Western community in Moscow and our apartment block was to be its core, every day of our lives a chapter. Suicides — we once saw a woman in a sari plunge to her death — surveillance, domestic dramas, defections . . .

Below we often heard a man screaming. I traced the screams to an apartment and tried to find out who occupied it. According to the UPKD it was empty. I asked Dima if he had heard the screams but he looked at me as though I was about to have a nervous breakdown. But Diane had heard them too.

One day we saw an ambulance draw up in the courtyard far below. A stretcher bearing a blanket-covered figure was carried from the entrance to the block; the ambulance departed and we heard no more screams.

What other dramas, unseen and unheard, were being enacted in other apartments? Every time I slotted a sheet of paper in my typewriter I opened a door. Every time I entered the shuddering elevator and shared it with another tenant, German, American, Scandinavian, Indian or Cuban, I was rubbing shoulders with the stuff of fiction.

Once I inadvertently created a chapter in the elevator. Diane and I with half a dozen friends were on our way down to a party in a Swedish journalist's flat when I accidently pressed the stop button. When I pressed the button to restart the machinery nothing happened. I pressed all the other buttons; nothing happened.

We were suspended in space and no one knew how far from the ground we were. I hammered on the sides of the elevator. It swayed but there were no answering cries from rescuers. I pressed the emergency button again with minimal hope: it was usually impossible to summon the caretaker on the telephone let alone from a lift.

After ten minutes the air started to become fetid and one of the girls was whimpering hysterically. This was understandable because if we were lodged equidistantly between floors there was little chance that anyone would hear us. Moreover, tenants were used to the lifts breaking down and screams were no strangers to the block.

I battered the sides of the cabin again. It swayed, more violently this time. It had never impressed me as a model of safety. How far above the ground were we? I imagined strands of steel rope parting, heard our screams as we plummeted to our deaths.

We were by now labouring for breath. I asked if anyone had a penknife; a West German journalist handed me one and I managed to prise back a flap of metal from the door. Fresh air flowed in. I shouted through the gap. Faintly we heard a reply. "Where are you?"

"Up here," I shouted, reflecting that this was a classically silly answer to a silly question.

Twenty minutes later a Russian rescue team arrived. They forced the doors and we tumbled out. We were about six inches above the level of the first floor.

*　　*　　*

Soon after this the Six Day War between Israel and the Arabs broke out and, in common with other correspondents, I was bombarded with queries about Soviet reaction to the Jewish aggression.

The unofficial reaction from my Russian contacts was surprising. They admired the Jews, they said, because of their enterprise and, in particular, their courage against the odds.

The Arabs? They shrugged eloquently. Officially, of course, they condemned the action of the 'bandit Israelis.'

The war made me restless for the first time since my arrival in Moscow. I imagined *Expressmen* descending on Tel Aviv and Cairo and conniving their way to the fighting; I remembered the cameraderie engendered by hostilities in Africa, India, Cyprus, Algeria . . . And here I was gathering a few quotes about Soviet intent and staring morosely at the chattering Tass machine recounting its masters' version of the fighting.

At midnight on the first day of the fighting the machine, half buried in serpentine coils of paper, stopped chattering and I went to bed. As I undressed I imagined reporters berating censors, furtively dispatching copy by couriers, hijacking Telex machines . . . I heard the gunfire and tasted warm beer in some bullet-riddled desert shack. These were the journalists who tomorrow would have their stories gloriously splashed across the front pages.

At 1 a.m. the Tass machine woke up. I blundered down the corridor to see what it had to say. And there spilling out from it was the first official Kremlin statement on the war. I tore off the copy, raced into the office and picked up the floating call from the *Express* in London.

Within a couple of minutes I was dictating: *Russia early today demanded that Israel should 'immediately and unconditionally' stop fighting and withdraw 'beyond the truce line'.*

The story was the front page lead.

Only then did I feel sorry for the reporters in the field. And a little guilty.

*   *   *

Unhappily for the British community the Queen's birthday coincided with the Six Day War. And because the Kremlin, albeit half-heartedly, was accusing Britain of supporting the Israelis, it looked as though the celebrations at the Embassy might have some taut undertones.

It is on this occasion in any capital city in the world that the British really come into their own. Union Jacks snap in the breeze, medals chink on chests like small change in the pocket, the imitation fruit on the ladies' bonnets glistens more invitingly than the strawberries with the cream. The Embassy becomes a microcosm of British insularity and once more, as we lift a gin-and-tonic or a weak whisky-and-soda from a butler's tray, we are empire builders.

At first it rained and we were herded into the Embassy building, once the home of a sugar baron, to watch the fat, summer drops of rain dribbling down the windows. Across the river we could see the spires and domes of the Kremlin. Almost as soon as I joined the sweating throng I was drawn into the Middle East controversy.

"So," said a towering Nigerian wearing ceremonial Army uniform, "what do you think about the Israelis' bandit agression?"

"I haven't had time to form any definite opinions yet," I said.

"I don't believe you," said the Nigerian, commendably outright.

"That's your privilege."

"You think it is the Arab's fault?"

"I think Israel may have been provoked."

"Bullshit," said the Nigerian, contemptuously tossing aside the language of diplomacy.

I shrugged, grabbed a drink and searched the room for salvation.

The Nigerian said: "You English have always been the aggressors. Why can you not recognise aggression when you see it?"

Suddenly inspired I said: "Have you ever been to Israel?"

He frowned. "No, but what has that got to do with it?"

"At least I've been there," I told him sternly, "and I must be in a better position to judge the situation than you."

"Bullshit —" he began, but I was saved by the weather. It had stopped raining and we were asked to adjourn to the garden.

Outside, the air smelled of wet dust; raindrops jewelled the shrubbery and somewhere in the foliage a bird sung.

I guided Diane firmly away from the Nigerian to the periphery of Sir Geoffrey Harrison's group. The subject under discussion was still Israel but the Ambassador was handling all questions with professional non-commitment.

It was left to Diane to provide a diversion. She had been devouring sausage-rolls as a prelude to strawberries-and-cream when Sir Geoffrey proposed the Queen.

"The Queen," we all chorused raising our glasses. Everyone, that is, except Diane who was unable either to speak or drink because her mouth was crammed with sausage-roll.

Sir Geoffrey eyed her speculatively for a moment before informing our group that it would be better to delay the toast until Diane could cope. Whereupon she began to chew frantically but, as she told me later, nerves had so dried up her saliva that it was like trying to eat three dry biscuits in two minutes at a church fête. When she had finally disposed of a sufficient quantity of sausage-roll to participate we concluded the royal salutation.

After that no more politics, no more bandit aggression. Was it, we debated, the first time a toast to a reigning monarch had been delayed by a mouthful of sausage-roll?

167

XVI

It was during this period, while world opinion was focused on the Middle East, that I made contact with a group of dissidents.

The Soviet attitude towards dissidence was at the time unpredictable. Such was the lingering confusion following Khrushchev's denunciation of Stalin that no one was sure whether they should deify or vilify such rebel intellectuals as Solzhenitsyn and Sakharov.

Solzhenitsyn, for instance, had been sent to a labour camp in 1945. But in 1962 he had been allowed to publish *One Day in the life of Ivan Denisovich*, the officially approved account of the misery endured in one of those establishments.

What then was the current Kremlin view of Russia's greatest man of letters since Tolstoy? At least the authorities were unequivocal on one point: if it *was* decided that a particular act of defiance was harmful to the State then the punishments were savage. Only the previous year two authors, Andrei Sinyavsky and Yuli Daniel, had been sent to a camp for publishing their works outside the Soviet Union and for writing without permits.

Whenever we Western journalists visited the Soviet Writers' Union we subjected officials and members to a barrage of questions about the future of the two incarcerated writers. In some cases the reaction was one of genuine perplex-

168

ity. If these men had libelled the State then surely they should pay the penalty?

Such sincerity was, perhaps, naïve but it did seem to me that it reflected an attitude rarely considered by the critics of Russia: that there were people of integrity who honestly believed that defamation of their country was a crime that should be severely punished. Sadly such encounters at the Writers' Union, initially enlightened, usually degenerated into slanging matches when Party hacks intervened.

From time to time *samizdat* — underground literature — found its way onto my doormat, delivered by some anonymous courier. Some of it was wild stuff; some of it consisted of pleas for the release of incarcerated prisoners; a lot of it concerned the plight of the Jews in the Soviet Union.

The Jewish *samizdat* condemned the exhausting and humiliating procedures that Jews who wanted to emigrate to Israel had to endure: it was but a trickle compared with the deluge of protest that was to follow the resurgence of Zionism after the defeat of the Arabs in the Six Day War. Such subversive literature rarely produced a news story but I more than most correspondents identified with it because I, too, was engaged in similar clandestine activities.

Perhaps if my manuscript were discovered I might be accused of disseminating 'falsehoods derogatory to the Soviet State and social system' and find myself in a position where, in my dotage, I would also be in a position to write a firsthand description of conditions in a labour camp.

*　　*　　*

My dissidents were hardly of the calibre of Solzhenitsyn or Sakharov but nonetheless they were an endangered species.

The call came one sultry evening while the Tass machine was clattering gamely away in the disused kitchen and the first

169

heavy drops of rain on the windows were heralding a summer storm.

The telephone rang and a woman's voice said: "If you want a good story stand near the flower-seller on Sovietskaya Square at ten o'clock this evening."

The line went dead.

"Who was it?" Diane asked.

"God knows," I replied and told her what the woman had said.

"Do you think you should go?"

"I haven't any choice," I told her.

"It could be a trap."

I handed her my manuscript. "Just look after this."

At 9.30 I put on a raincoat, picked up an umbrella and strode heroically out of the apartment. Bruised clouds hung low in the sky and thunder grumbled in the distance; rain bounced ankle-high in the puddles.

I drove past the guards, waving at them with theatrical bravado, and headed down Kutuzovsky towards the centre of the city, tyres throwing up wings of spray.

Whatever lay ahead there was no hope of nocturnal concealment. The White Nights were upon us and, although darkness wasn't totally shouldered aside as it was further north, the night consisted of an hour or so of twilight until dawn broke green-rimmed on the horizon.

I parked the Cortina, paddled round the small square which reminded me of the artists' quarter of Paris, and took up position just to the left of the flower-seller whose blooms were protected from the deluge by a tarpaulin roof.

The danger was that the call from the anonymous woman would have been monitored and, although I was fairly sure I hadn't been followed, it was a simple operation to mount surveillance on the flower-stall.

I looked around. There were half a dozen or so people in the

170

square, waiting beneath umbrellas or fleeing, heads bowed, from the rain. If some *agent provocateur* suddenly thrust an inflammatory document into my hand it would be a simple matter to jump me.

I glanced at my wristwatch. It was ten o'clock. Lightning leaped across the sky, thunder cracked. The flower-seller began to gather up the blossoms on her stall. Five more minutes passed. I began to suspect that I was the victim of a Gilbert Lewthwaite practical joke. Then a young man hunched in a raincoat bumped into me, murmured, "First turning on the right, second doorway," and walked on.

As I reached the doorway a black Volga pulled up. The rear door opened and a woman's voice said: "Jump in and be quick about it."

The car took off as I tumbled in, slamming the door behind me. Beside me sat a slender girl with sea-green eyes and severely trimmed blonde hair; the driver who was in his early twenties wore a jaunty blue cap.

"Good evening," I said inadequately.

The girl didn't reply; instead she stared at me as though photographing and filing me.

The driver said over his shoulder: "So you're Derek Lambert," as if I didn't quite measure up.

"That's right," I said, "and who the hell are you?" reflecting that they were, perhaps, members of an execution squad.

"A free man," he replied.

"Then why all the secrecy?"

He didn't reply but the car skidded viciously around a corner and accelerated down a straight road that looked like a canal.

At last the girl spoke. "You're right, of course" — it was the voice on the telephone — "he's not free. Nor am I. Nor are any of us. But we are not slaves."

"Where are we going?" I asked.

"To a party," she replied.

Whereupon the driver swung the Volga into a maze of narrow streets. We stopped outside a brown painted door; the girl climbed out of the car and knocked — three quick taps, three slow, three quick. The door opened and the girl beckoned me inside.

We went down a flight of steps to a cellar door. Faintly I could hear the sound of music. Another coded knock and the door opened, closing swiftly as we were hustled inside. The cellar was spacious, its walls plastered with posters promoting anything from Coca Cola to bullfights. In one corner couples were dancing to Beatles records; in another an ancient copying machine was spewing out sheets of paper printed in muzzy purple ink.

Elsewhere young people were playing chess, debating, consuming soft drinks, reading . . . a few were necking. I might have been in a youth club anywhere in New York or London.

The girl who said her name was Sonia introduced me to some of her friends; in each case the response was friendly but wary.

"Would you like a drink?" Sonia asked. And when she brought me a fizzy cherryade: "So, what do you think?"

"It looks great," I told her, "but I still don't understand why you had to be so secret. Are you plotting to blow up the Kremlin?"

Sonia who wore a grey dress and a pearl necklace gestured around her. "It's very simple. All this is against the law. We don't have permission to hold such gatherings." A smile illuminated her small stern features. "And we certainly don't have permission to play the Beatles or dance like that," pointing at a couple jiving.

We sat down at a table beside two men becalmed in a game of chess. What, I asked her, was the message being pumped out by the copying machine.

172

"It's not a message," she said, crossing shapely legs. "It's our magazine. But we do publish comments that would never be printed in the official Press."

"Such as?"

"Reviews of music, art, literature."

"Anything against the State?"

She considered this, sipping her drink through a pink straw, before conceding: "Against the State yes, against the country no."

"What is your principal complaint against the State?"

No hesitation this time. "That we are not allowed to express our own opinions. That even our minds are not our own — or so they believe."

"Aren't you afraid of being caught down here?"

She nodded. "Of course. But we change our meeting places often. If we were raided I imagine all of us would be sent away for at least three years."

"And you think it's worth the risk?"

"Obviously," she said. "We don't want to grow up like our parents — puppets."

Finishing my drink, I gazed around trying to retain the scene for the future. It was young, brave, sad — and bizarre. Comparable to a group of students in an English university town living under the threat of imprisonment for publishing some absurdity in the Rag Week magazine.

I reminded her that on the telephone she had mentioned a story.

She was surprised. "But this is the story," she said. "The fact that we exist. We want the West to know that the young people of the Soviet Union are not tame rabbits."

I pointed out that if I wrote a feature about the gathering they would all be in trouble, but she seemed unperturbed.

"I'll see what I can do," I told her as the door closed and the rhythm of the Beatles "Yeah, yeah, yeah," faded behind us.

When we emerged into the street the black Volga swept up, tyres skidding on the wet surface. The driver took me back to Sovietskaya Square without speaking, deposited me on the corner and disappeared at speed.

I put up my umbrella and made my way through the rain to the waiting Cortina. Back at the apartment I put my finger to my lips and pointed at Fred's light fitting when Diane asked me what had happened.

"It was Gilbert," I said. "He just wanted a drink."

"Just one drink?" Diane asked, born actress that she was.

"Well, one or two. Maybe three," I said.

Next morning I telephoned Novosti with a routine query to a feature story. As I was about to hang up the man on the other end of the line said: "By the way, Gaspadeen Lambert, how did you enjoy the Beatles?"

XVII

After covering the Middle East war by remote control I collaborated with Bill Lovelace on a series of features.

We met gorgeous girls on the Black Sea beaches to prove that not all Soviet women were built like weight-lifters. We put together a story about a mongrel dog named Vesna that had been drowned deliberately for forty minutes and brought to life again in the interests of scientific research. We reported a wedding in Odessa Cathedral which, contrary to our preconceived notions, was packed . . .

In the evenings Diane and I wandered around the city streets and parks immersed in their summer languor. The gentle Lenin Hills, the Ferris wheel in Gorky Park like the fly-wheel of a watch in the distance, the dusty soldiers and their dimpled girls, the ice-cream and *kvas* vendors, and the dazed families from the provinces visiting their capital.

Sometimes we strolled around the grounds of the Kremlin which, with its green roofs, mellow walls and golden domes, looked no more sinister than Hampton Court on a Bank Holiday.

Sightseers were allowed to visit three-quarters of this august complex surrounded by fifty-foot high walls; the remainder where the Soviet leaders tried to direct the destiny of the world was sealed off by guards.

But it was difficult on these serene evenings to comprehend

the awesome decisions taken beyond those guards. The scent of flowers was heavy, the influence of the old white-stone cathedrals benign.

We visited the Kremlin Palace, the Arsenal, Ivan the Great's Bell Tower and, incorrigible tourists that we were, the Tsar Cannon and the towering Tsar Bell which in the eighteenth century took two years to cast.

At other times we ferreted among second-hand shops in burrowing streets behind the pseudo-Gothic skyscrapers built by Stalin — not as horrendous as the architectural aesthetes would have you believe — grubbing around for icons or brass candelabra or chandeliers with dust-caked tears torn from the home of some long dead aristocrat.

Alongside men in white shirts and dark trousers and their wives blossoming in the latest batch of print frocks to reach the stores, we paraded the broad avenues, discovered squares lost in dusty green sleep, lingered beside the stunned river.

And when we returned home and opened the door of the apartment there was still a microcosm of summer to be savoured. The air smelled of the carnations brought by Valentina; the net curtains billowed gently in the breeze; and somewhere there I sensed childhood.

But all too soon we smelled the premature, chestnut scents of autumn. A time of change . . . But I wasn't prepared for the changes, as bizarre and dramatic as the events on my Moscow baptismal, that were to follow.

*   *   *

The débâcle began with a twinge of pain in one knee at lunchtime. Deciding that I may have sprained it dancing at a party I lay down on the bed to rest it. When I awoke from a doze, the knee was throbbing with pain. I tried to get off the bed but collapsed in agony.

176

By the following morning the pain had spread to the other knee and both ankles. While Valentina and Dima crept around the apartment as though in the presence of death, Diane called the doctor at the British Embassy.

He was a small dark man with a unique bedside manner. He opened the proceedings by sitting on one of my blanket-covered knees and seemed perturbed when I punched him off howling like a doomed animal entering the slaughter-house.

After making a routine examination he produced a weighty medical manual, made himself comfortable on the edge of the bed and said brightly: "Now let's see if we can find out what's the matter."

Together we consulted the book alternately nodding when we thought we had nailed the ailment and shaking our heads when we came upon some contradictory symptom such as enlarged testicles.

"How are they by the way?" he asked.

"Fine thank you," I told him, giving them a little pat.

He took a blood sample, prescribed aspirin and departed. The sepulchral faces of Dima and Valentina hovered at the door to the bedroom. Would I be 'phoning London? Dima asked. I shook my head. "Tell the stringer (a reporter on UPI) to cover for us," I told him.

I lunched on aspirins and tea and, between jabs of pain, dozed, vaguely aware of Diane tiptoeing around the room. By the evening I had developed a fever and the patterns on the peeling green wallpaper were malevolent figures beckoning me to Hades.

A night of pain and fevered dreams followed. In the morning the doctor arrived with the news that I was suffering from rheumatic fever.

"Is that bad?" I asked struggling up from the pillows.

He pushed me firmly back. "You mustn't move," he said.

"Never?"

"Any movement affects the heart."

At this intelligence my heart began to thud audibly.

Valentina arrived wearing black and Dima's apparel seemed even more sombre than usual. They had presumably left their wreaths outside the door. The doctor prescribed a phenomenal dosage of aspirin and departed cheerily with the observation that "we should just have to wait and see."

Of the three other occupants of the apartment only Diane behaved as though little untoward had occurred. She busied herself about the place, poured me gallons of orange juice, shovelled aspirins down my throat and beat me repeatedly at Scrabble. True love it transparently was because she also emptied my bedpan, triumphantly holding it aloft like a waiter with a tray in a crowded restaurant.

On the third day Vladimir arrived, fresh air following in his wake, his predatory face glowing with good health. A depressing spectacle for one who waggled his toes at his peril.

He had presumably heard about my plight through Dima, Valentina or Fred. He brought flowers and grapes and steaks from a moose that he had shot over the weekend; at the thought of chewing those steaks, as tough as plimsolls, my heart gave a warning thud or two.

He sat on the edge of the bed and said: "As is well known Soviet hospitals are the best in the world."

I made some guarded reply.

"*We* think," said Vladimir, "that you should go to a hospital here in Moscow where you will have the benefit of our wonderful medical services."

It was a frightening proposition.

"It's very good of you," I said, "but . . ."

"I have an ambulance standing by," Vladimir said helpfully.

"If I move I'll need a hearse," I said.

"A horse?"

"No, a hearse."

178

I explained laboriously. He nodded thoughtfully and, turning to Diane, remarked: "He has a fever, yes?"

"I think he should stay here," Diane said firmly.

Vladimir stood up. "I understand," he said stiffly. And to me: "Anything you want please telephone me. A little vodka perhaps?"

Firmly Diane led him to the door.

As he turned to say goodbye I asked him: "Vladimir, what did the reporter say when he was charged by a wild moose?"

Perplexed, Vladimir shook his head.

"No moose is good moose," I told him.

As he walked down the corridor I heard him saying to Diane: "He is a little demented, yes?"

Diane's reply was inaudible.

Lying there in bed with the Soviet media to hand — black-and-white television and scattered newspapers and magazines — I realised how secrecy rooted deep in history still pervades the country.

Every evening I switched on the thirty-minute news cast, and became the acknowledged western authority on the machine-tool production figures in the Ukraine, the grain harvest, the latest space shot and the itinerary of the current leader of a satellite Communist country meeting his masters.

Anti-American demonstrations anywhere in the world received ample coverage as did the slightest hint of anything critical about West Germany. (East Germans were cast in the heroic mould).

Nothing reflecting adversely on Russia was ever shown because obviously it never occurred. No riots, no crime, no strikes, no plane crashes . . . to see even a glimmer of the truth you had to scan the Russian newspapers with an expert eye. Then you might discover a two-line item, squashed between a denunciation of the latest Chinese treachery and encouraging coal figures in Siberia, revealing that an airliner with a hundred passengers on board had crashed or that bubonic plague had devastated the Crimea.

If a Russian relied on the media then, quite simply, nothing ever happened. But few Russians bought that: they merely accepted their heritage of secrecy and tried to fill in the gaps. Better still, they listened to the BBC or the Voice of America. The rest of the television programmes flickering at the end of my bed were as predictable as the news: opera, ballet, circus and movies about World War II.

And sport. For this I forgave a lot. Almost every night I watched a football match; I was there inside the box and, as an empty goal presented itself, lashed out with my right foot only to fall back on the pillows with a cry of pain as my knee reminded me that it was full of razor-blades.

When the set finally exploded with a blue flash one day I mourned the loss of the football but found that, on the whole, my recovery was accelerated by the absence of this entertainment and the news-that-never-was.

* * *

For five weeks I lay virtually motionless waiting for the pain to subside. And all the time I was worried by two possibilities: whether, like some forgotten spy, I was going to die a bleak death behind the Iron Curtain, and whether — assuming the first possibility proved groundless — I would be able to smuggle my embryonic manuscript out of the country.

The first priority with the manuscript was to hide it because I had little doubt that, one day while Diane was shopping, a routine search of my office would be carried out. I solved this problem by tucking it under my bedpan, a receptacle that, I reasoned, would deter the most diligent of investigators.

Meanwhile I continued to correspond in code with

180

Desmond Elliott and the state of health of Uncle Albert, who had returned from his cruise, was the subject of far more solicitous discussion than my own. In the evenings I managed to do some work on the book, capturing while I could the atmosphere of our concrete island and its diverse inhabitants.

But how would I get the manuscript through emigration, assuming, as the doctor had indicated, that I would have to fly back to London for further medical tests and that I would be taken to the aircraft in a wheelchair?

I saw myself sitting helplessly in the chair while a customs officer scanned the opening pages, regarded me through slitted eyes and made a telephone call. Then I would be wheeled away to oblivion. I brooded thus as I lay gazing through the window watching autumn clouds assembling on the horizon.

After a while I was taken off a diet of gruel and beef broth and allowed my first light snack. A beaming Valentina obliged enthusiastically. I imagined she would poach an egg or, perhaps, rustle up an omelette. Instead she laid in front of me two vegetable marrows stuffed with meat and tied with string. Her concern was touching, her motives unsubtle: she took home with her any food that we left uneaten and that night she departed with one stuffed and unopened marrow in her basket.

Twice a day Dima presented himself at my bedside with his work reports. He still clipped newspapers and magazines, tended the Tass machine and passed on messages to the Foreign Deskmen who had reacted sympathetically to my illness. But I suspected that, in my absence, the Big Hairy Beast was getting more than his fair share of attention.

Visits from Gilbert Lewthwaite and John Miller brightened the days. But the most pleasant times were after a Valentina 'snack' when Diane and I played scrabble or chess.

Only once did I have a misunderstanding with Valentina.

One Sunday she cooked a roast joint, carved it with a magician's flourish and said: "Well, what do you think?"

Insensitively I replied: "It's just a roast, isn't it?"

Whereupon she stalked from the room and didn't return for the rest of the day. Only much later did I discover that it was the first roast she had ever cooked.

On the sixth week I was allowed to get up. But, as I could barely bend my knees, I had to use a stick, lumbering unsteadily around the apartment like Frankenstein. A couple of days later Gilbert drove Diane and me to the top of the Lenin Hills. There spread below us was Moscow pinned to the ground by the spike of the Ostankino television tower.

A breeze climbed the hills, the sun shone from a pale sky and, as I walked and laughed, I smelled and heard nuances of life buried since my teens: fragrances of promise and regret, a fluted note of birdsong, summer and autumn smokily melding.

When I had recovered sufficiently to be flown back to London for further medical treatment I threw a muted farewell party and announced that I would be back soon. However, I knew myself that I was now saying goodbye to Russia for ever and everyone accepted this for the lie it was.

Vladimir, Dima and Valentina gave Diane and me presents, Vladimir another box exquisitely painted in scarlet, green and gold which stands on my desk today. The picture on the box was, of course, a hunting scene.

Despite the creed they served they were three of the most loyal friends I have ever had. And because of that creed, I knew I would never see them again. Never again submerge in one of Valentina's breathtaking embraces, never again trace the lineage of the Abominable Snowman with Dima and watch a smile transform that earnest face as he uncovered fresh evidence of the creature's existence, never again denounce blood sports to Vladimir as the fire-water flushed his alert, outdoor face and inflamed his words.

I bid less emotional farewells to Gilbert Lewthwaite and John Miller and their wives because journalists always meet again.

When they were all gone and Diane and I were alone with the past, a year of it to the day, we stood at the window gazing down at the sparse evening traffic and up at the stars assembling in the darkening sky.

And for a moment I wanted to see another winter through. I remembered not the razored wind cutting across Red Square: I remembered instead that indoors it had been as snug as hot-buttered toast beside a coal fire. We pulled the curtains and our year thickened around us. But there was something wrong, a discord in the memories.

It was Diane who identified it. She pointed under the television set. The sugar-coated redcurrant had disappeared.

*   *   *

Our departure was abrupt. There were the exit visas, there were the air tickets, there was the cheque for the money I had saved at the bank. The door of the apartment closed behind us, the lift made its customary palsied descent, and then we were in a taxi on the way to Sheremetyevo Airport.

I had the manuscript of the opening chapters of the novel in my briefcase and I had devised a crude scheme to avoid detection. A wheelchair, I had decided, could well be my saviour because airport officials were more likely to concentrate on a patient's luggage than the patient himself. Feigning a relapse, I had requested a wheelchair — and planned to sit on the manuscript wrapped up in a copy of *Pravda*.

As we approached the airport my agitation increased as I envisaged British Embassy Press briefings of the future.

Lewthwaite: "Any further news of Lambert, sir?"

Ambassador: "Nothing fresh. As far as we know he's still carving chess pieces."

Miller: "Any firm date for his release?"

Ambassador, yawning: "Not a thing. It rather looks as though he'll have to serve his full ten years."

Just before we reached the airport I removed the manuscript from my briefcase. The wheelchair was waiting outside the departure lounge. As I sat down I slid the *Pravda*-covered folder beneath me.

A customs officer made a perfunctory search of one of my suitcases, then stared speculatively at the wheelchair. I smiled bravely at him and clutched my knee. He waved me through.

A stewardess helped me up the steps to the TU-104 commenting that it was gratifying to note that I appreciated *Pravda* so much that I was taking a copy home with me. As I settled down in my seat I reflected that any novel that had spent its formative chapters beneath a bedpan and its creator's backside deserved to be published.

From the window of the plane I gazed down at the city, basking in the sunshine, which a year ago had seemed so daunting. But I had found within its confines a sense of security compounded in part by bravado, domestic contentment and a stimulating professional life.

My emotions as the city faded forever from my sight were as muddled as a fevered dream. But all the swirling impressions were tethered to a central pivot of regret that so much of the antagonism between the West and the Soviet Union was based on misconception.

In the West I subsequently encountered total disbelief that the Russian people could actually be happy; when I protested that, for the most part, they were, and that they now possessed more material benefits than they had ever owned in their history, they reacted as though I had been turned.

What the pundits fail to appreciate is that the driving force behind the Russians is patriotism and they will endure any privations imposed by the State to keep its flame burning. Equally they cannot conceive that anyone living under the yoke of Capitalism can find contentment. How can they when their daily fare is violence, unemployment, industrial chaos?

Certainly Communism as we know it today doesn't work. But then neither does democracy when we have reached the point where its principles are unscrupulously exploited.

At the moment, however, democracy still has the edge. We still enjoy freedom and in Russia that is an unattainable commodity which you cannot even buy in the *beryozka* shops.

*　　*　　*

I had by now decided to leave journalism seventeen years after joining the *Dartmouth Chronicle* and try to earn a living as a novelist.

I presented myself to Desmond Elliott with a battered *Uncle Albert* in my hand and he gave me the encouraging news that, on the strength of my autobiography, *The Sheltered Days*, about life as an evacuee in World War II, both Michael Joseph in London and Coward-Macann in New York had agreed to give me advances on my novel.

I resigned from the *Express*, forever grateful for the opportunities for writing they and the *Daily Mirror* had given me, and, with Diane, took myself to the Irish village of Ballycotton.

Before departing I was examined by a Harley Street specialist.

"Did you have blood tests in Russia?" he asked.

I nodded.

"Well they must have got them muddled up," he said.

A clammy finger of fear touched me.

He scribbled a prescription and, with a final indecipherable flourish, asked: "Do you know what was really wrong with you in Moscow, Mr Lambert?"

I shook my head forlornly.

"You had gout," he said.

It seemed apt. In the first year of my career I had been ingloriously fired from the *Dartmouth Chronicle* for reporting a case of chicken-pox as an outbreak of small-pox: now I was to bow out prodded by the pains of an ailment that is considered to be hilariously funny by those who have never suffered from it.

I thanked him and walked out into the sunlit street to begin a new life.